CHAMPIONSHIP WRESTLING

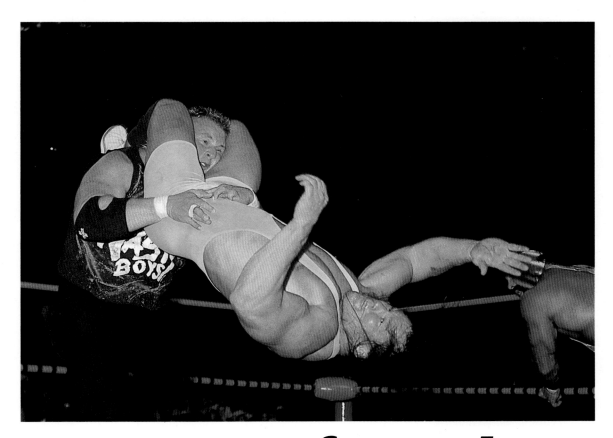

Masters of Mayhem

CHAMPIONSHIP WRESTLING

Masters of Mayhem

GEORGE NAPOLITANO

MALLARD
PRESS

First published in the United States of
America in 1991 by The Mallard Press
Mallard Press and its accompanying design
and logo are trademarks of BDD
Promotional Book Company, Inc.

ISBN 0-7924-5595-9

Printed in Hong Kong

ACKNOWLEDGMENTS

This book would not have been possible were it not
for the help of many people. I wish to thank them
for their support and assistance: Steve Weitzen,
Gary Juster, Sal Ivone, John and Roberta Bohan,
Ben Sacks, Bob Sacks, Freddie Colon, Ray Dar-
iano, Mike Allen, Blackjack Brown, The Slammer,
Steve Ciacciarelli, Michael Benson, John Arezzi,
Jack O'Brien, Scott Record, Jody McDonald, Koi-
chi Yoshizawa, Jim Herd, Mario Savoldi, Jim Ross,
Robert ·D'Onfrio, Michael Fleming, Max Sabrin,
Greg Posella, Joji Inoue, and the staff at Hanover
Communications, Inc. in New York City.

PAGE 1: *Scott Steiner catches Brian
Knobbs in the devastating move
that he invented, the
Frankensteiner.*

PAGES 2-3: *Nature Boy Ric Flair
and the Total Package Lex Luger
are locked up in the dreaded
figure-four leg-lock.*

BELOW: *Mirror, mirror on the wall,
who is the meanest of them all?
Why, Road Warrior Hawk, of
course!*

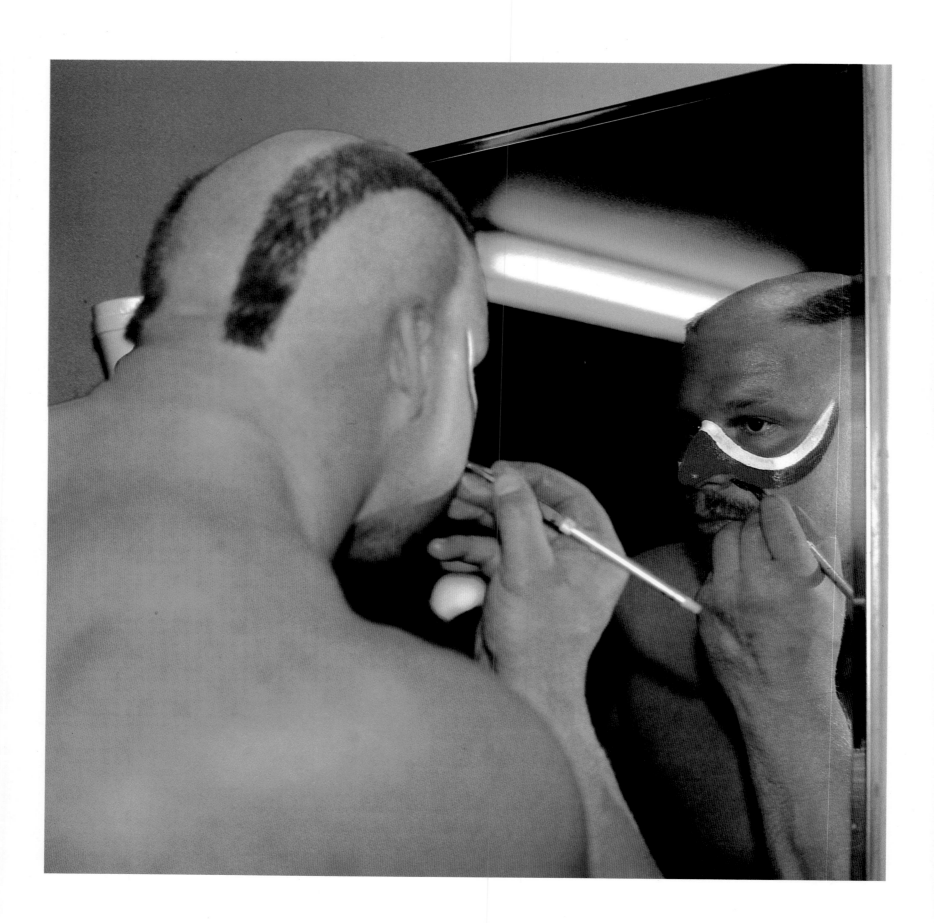

CONTENTS

INTRODUCTION

Wrestling has a long and illustrious history. Although the wrestling that we see on television today is full of glitz, glamour, pathos and comedy, its roots can be traced back to ancient Greece. Wrestling was even one of the first Olympic sports. Many people, however, don't equate Olympic-style wrestling with the television variety, but there is a definite connection between the two. In fact, many of today's stars receive their wrestling education in the amateur ranks, and several actually wrestled in the Olympics.

Wrestling as we know it today is far removed from the sport the ancient Greeks practiced. Sure the premise is the same, but that's where the similarity ends. Wrestling today is a human soap opera, and its cast of stars includes every character imaginable. Old time "purists" may be appalled at what has happened to their beloved sport today. Actually all the characters and situations, the glamour and showmanship, are just a 1990s way of presenting the same things that have been big during the past four decades.

I have been closely following the sport as a photographer, editor and author since 1971, and in this time I have seen quite a few major changes. But looking back, I realize that the core and spirit of wrestling actually remains the same. The old saying "what goes around comes around" definitely applies to wrestling.

The biggest difference I have noticed in the past 20 years is the proliferation of the musclemen that now rule the sport. In the early days big, fat, beefy men dominated the industry. The biggest man in the fifties and sixties was Happy Humphrey, who tipped the scales at over 700 pounds. Not far behind was Haystacks Calhoun from Morgans Corner, Arkansas, who weighed in at 601 pounds. The vast majority weighed between 225 and 350 pounds, and very few, with the exception of Gene "Mr. America" Stanlee, exhibited well-defined musculature. Today this is no longer the exception, but the rule. To make it to the top a wrestler has to be well conditioned and in fighting shape. The change in body style started to take hold in the mid-seventies with Superstar Billy Graham. With his flowing blond locks and 24-inch pythons, Graham was the man from whom Hulk Hogan copied his entire style and persona. If cable TV had been around in Graham's day, he would have been

the superstar – instead of the Hulkster – to become the idol of millions.

When I first became involved in the sport, wrestling was regional in scope. The wrestling world, as defined by insiders, was divided into territories. There was the WWWF (World Wide Wrestling Federation) in the Northeast. Its boundaries extended from Washington, D.C. to Maine. There was the Mid-Atlantic Region, which was an affiliate of the NWA (National Wrestling Association) and covered the states of Virginia, North Carolina and South Carolina. Florida was also an NWA affiliate, and wrestling matches were held weekly in Jacksonville, Miami, Orlando and Fort Lauderdale. The Central States Promotion was an NWA affiliate in Missouri and Kansas, with the famed Keil Auditorium in St. Louis the site of many NWA title changes.

Texas had its own promotion, and fans could always count on seeing the wildest and craziest matches in the Lone Star State. Weekly cards were held in Dallas, San Antonio, Corpus Christi and at the Sam Houston Coliseum in Houston. The Californian cities of San Bernadino, Sacramento and Los Angeles were also big wrestling meccas. The L.A. Olympic Auditorium was the West Coast's answer to New York's Madison Square Garden.

The American Wrestling Association was another main organization. The AWA, headquartered in Minneapolis, Minnesota, promoted throughout the states of Iowa, Nebraska, North and South Dakota, Colorado, Utah, Nevada and parts of California. In addition there were many other promotions scattered throughout the country where one could expect to see plenty of action and excitement.

Throughout the seventies and into the eighties I regularly attended matches in every of the aforementioned cities. Every year I made certain to travel the loop, photographing and interviewing the stars who were champions in every part of the country. I found the Texas and Florida promotions to be two of my favorite areas to cover. They had great talent and exciting action.

Today, due to the popularity of wrestling on cable, network and satelite TV, the sport has become national – even international – in scope. Fans sitting at home in Portland, Oregon, can see the same stars that fans watch in Portland, Maine!

ABOVE: *The Hulkster boarding a plane for a flight to another city, another title defense, and as is his custom, another victory!*

Wrestling no longer has that hometown flavor. Regional favorites are a thing of the past. In fact, shows at the small local arenas are infrequently held. Large arena shows and TV spectaculars are the rule today.

As most fans of the mat sport are aware, there are two main wrestling organizations today: the WWF (World Wrestling Federation) and the NWA (National Wrestling Alliance). Smaller groups which challenge the larger leagues also exist, such as the GWF (Global Wrestling Federation) and the ICW (International Championship Wrestling).

Today's young fans know very little about the way wrestling was prior to the emergence of Hulk Hogan and the beginning of Wrestlemanias. Men like Frank Gotch, George Hackenschmidt, Strangler Lewis, Lou Thesz, Gorgeous George, Pat O'Connor, Buddy Rogers, Bruno Sammartino, Verne Gagne, Chief Jay Strongbow, Ivan Putski, Pedro Morales, Nick Bockwinkel and Superstar Billy Graham are the ones to whom such stars as Hulk Hogan, Sting, the Ultimate Warrior, Ric Flair, Dusty Rhodes, Mr. Perfect, Ricky Steam-

boat, and count-less others owe a debt of gratitude for laying the foundation of a very rewarding and lucrative profession.

This book tells the story, in words and pictures, of wrestling today. It depicts the stars in all their glory, giving fans a feel for what wrestling is all about. I will take you behind closed doors into the private sanctuaries of the locker rooms, and into the ringside seats of many famous arenas. You will see it all – from the high-flying maneuvers to the colorful costumes – just as I see it through the lens of my Nikon cameras. Welcome to the wild and wacky world of professional wrestling.

See you at the matches.

George Napolitano

George Napolitano

CHAPTER ONE

THE SUPERSTARS

Hulk Hogan

There are dozens of stars in the wrestling business, but there are only a few bona fide superstars. Judging by fan reaction, I have selected those wrestlers who are the most colorful, controversial and charismatic.

The wrestling superstars in this chapter are members of an elite group who have all made important contributions to the sport, and who will continue to dominate the wrestling world in the future.

You cannot talk about superstardom without citing Hulk Hogan first and foremost. He is the man who almost single-handedly led wrestling into the modern era. Before the Hulk came along, wrestling fans kept their true feelings a secret. The Hulk changed all this and in the process made wrestling respectable.

The Hulk did it all. Arenas around the world set attendance records with the Hulk in the main event. The turning point came on March 31, 1985, during Wrestlemania I. From that day on, Wrestlemania and Hulk-a-Mania became almost synonymous. The Hulk's enormous popularity has helped the sport grow to new heights, reaching millions of new fans and elevating wrestling to an important position in the television, movie, magazine and sports industries.

Easily the most recognizable figure in the sport today, the native of Venice Beach, California, has clearly earned his superstar status. Hogan was 6'6" tall at Robinson High School in Tampa, Florida, and had the nickname Whitey. He showed a tremendous interest in sports and enjoyed the time he spent in the gym, where he worked on his body and developed the extremely muscular physique that is so familier today.

There are many versions as to how Hogan got his start in wrestling. Hogan has not clarified the actual details regarding his entrance into the wrestling business. Perhaps he feels that several people had a part in helping him along the way. It is a fact that former wrestler Jerry Brisco saw Hogan in a gym in Florida and was impressed with his massive size. Brisco suggested that Hogan consider entering wrestling.

Hulk was initially trained by Hiro Matsuda in Florida, and he made his debut in Georgia working under the ring name, Terry "The Hulk" Boulder. After a few months he began wrestling in the Tennessee promotion with the moniker, "Sterling Golden."

Wrestling manager Classy Freddie Blassie then brought him into the old WWF in 1979, where he became known as Hulk Hogan. Because of the Hulk's height, the rippling muscles on his 302-pound body, and the influence of notorious bad guy Blassie, at first Hulk Hogan wrestled as a villain.

After a short stay in the WWF, Hogan journeyed to the AWA Promotion in the Midwest, where he was managed by Luscious Johnny Valiant, who turned out to be another bad influence on the Hulk. Even though a villain, Hogan was winning all his matches and traveled to the Orient, where he was a huge success in Japan.

Back in the U.S. Hogan was called upon to act the role of the wrestler Thunder Lips in Sylvester Stallone's movie, *Rocky III*. Little did Hogan know that in a few more years he would be starring in his own movies!

Hogan's chance at the WWF World Title came

ABOVE: *A rare photo of a young Hulk Hogan with his former manager, Freddie Blassie. Note the chest hair shaved to look like an atomic bomb explosion!*

RIGHT: *The Hulkster looks to the crowd for inspiration, asking them to let him hear it!*

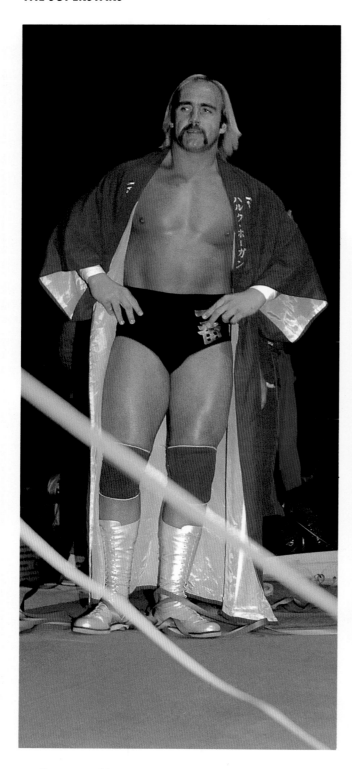

special when Ted DiBiase paid off an "evil twin" referee, who cheated and awarded the belt to the Giant. When the title position was declared vacant because of the foul deed, Wrestlemania IV featured a hard-fought tournament for the belt with the Macho Man Randy Savage winning the prestigious championship.

Hogan and Savage were friends and even Tag Team partners for a while. But the Macho Man viciously attacked Hogan, accusing him of "having jealous eyes" toward Savage's manager, Miss Elizabeth. The two former friends faced off at Wres-

on January 23, 1984 in Madison Square Garden against the Iron Sheik. Hogan did not squander the opportunity. In front of the packed house of over 20,000 fans, the Hulk escaped from the Sheik's camel clutch, delivered a leg drop and got the pin in less than seven minutes!

With Hogan as champion, the new era in professional wrestling began. The Hulk was now a hero to millions, and he used his fame to spread positive messages. He told his younger fans, "Say your prayers, eat your vitamins and stay in school."

Many bad guy wrestlers challenged the Hulkster. As the number one man in the WWF, he was confronted constantly by the most hated villains in wrestling. Starring in every Wrestlemania, the Hulkster proved to be the top box office attraction in the business.

At the first Wrestlemania he teamed with television star Mr. T to defeat Roddy Piper and Paul Orndorff. At Wrestlemania II he conquered the giant King Kong Bundy. At Wrestlemania III he topped Andre the Giant. The following year he lost his title to Andre the Giant on a international TV

tlemania V, with Hulk regaining the title.

As a battle between the good guys, Wrestlemania VI was called the "Ultimate Challenge." In the grueling match Hogan was defeated by the Ultimate Warrior.

Even though Hogan had lost the title, he did not lose any fans. He was just as popular as ever, and took some time off from the ring to film a series of movies. The fans did not want the Hulkster to leave wrestling, and after a massive outcry from the public, Hogan was back in the ring fighting off all comers.

In title challenges in countries around the world, including Japan, Australia, New Zealand, Great Britain, Germany, and Austria, the Hulkster has defeated the Earthquake, Sergeant Slaughter, the Undertaker and everybody who has ever attempted to bring him down.

All the experts expect Hogan to continue as the dominant star in wrestling whether he has the world title or not. There are definitely more world titles in the cards for the Hulkster. In between these new title reigns, he will still be the people's champ!

FAR LEFT: *Hulk prepares for a match in Japan. The big guy wears Japanese lettering on his ring robe and trunks out of respect for the great tradition that the wrestling sport has had in Japan.*

LEFT: *Hogan is the most popular wrestler of all time. He is always surrounded by fans who clamor for his autograph.*

RIGHT: *Hulk feels the pressure as the Ultimate Warrior applies a bear hug during their historic match at Wrestlemania VI. Hogan lost the belt that night, but regained it by beating America's Turncoat, Sergeant Slaughter, at the following Wrestlemania.*

The Ultimate Warrior

The Ultimate Warrior was a bodybuilder from New York who journeyed to Gold's Gym in Southern California, where he was discovered working out on the heavy weights by wrestling trainer Red Bastein. Bastein picked four young men to become "Power Team USA," a dream he had of an elite group that would dominate the wrestling world. Two of its original members left the business, but the Ultimate Warrior, who was known in his early days as Blade Runner Rock and then as the Dingo Warrior, and his partner, Flash, who later became known as Sting, both rose to world championships!

Ultimate stands 6'2″ tall and has an incredibly chiseled 265-pound body. His rookie year was spent in the Mid-South region, where he showed all the signs of future greatness. He traveled to the Texas territory, where he feuded with the one and only Rick Rude.

After joining the WWF he rose quickly to the top and established himself as a superstar when he defeated the Honky Tonk Man at Summer Slam to win the Intercontinental Title on August 29, 1988. As a fan favorite with a growing following, he feuded with Ted DiBiase, Haku, Rick Rude and Andre the Giant. He amazed everyone by beating Andre in several matches around the country in less than two minutes each time!

The pinnacle of his career came when he defeated Hulk Hogan in a scientific match at Wrestlemania VI, winning the World Title.

His powerful running clothesline and bone-crunching bearhug insure that the Ultimate Warrior will continue to be one of the superstars of the wrestling world for years to come.

ABOVE: *Before losing the World Title to Sergeant Slaughter at the Royal Rumble in February 1991, the Ultimate Warrior looked invincible. Don't worry, the Warrior will get his revenge!*

RIGHT: *The Warrior dons shades, but his vision is clear. He wants another championship belt to add to his previous titles.*

Ric Flair

The 6′ tall, 242-pound "Nature Boy" Ric Flair has been the dominant star in the National Wrestling Alliance. He captured its World Championship six different times through the 1980s and has shown that the 1990s might just be his decade too!

Considered by most experts to be one of the all-time greats when it comes to technical ability in the ring, he has often been a rulebreaker with a win-at-all-costs attitude – but who can argue with his success?

Originally from Minnesota, now residing in Charlotte, North Carolina, Flair was trained by Verne Gagne. He rose to prominence in the Mid-Atlantic area, where he showed signs of greatness during his early years.

He captured the NWA World Belt in 1981 defeating Dusty Rhodes in Kansas City. In the 10 years since then Flair has had monumental feuds with Harley Race, Kerry Von Erich, Dusty Rhodes, Ronnie Garvin, Ricky Steamboat and Sting. All these opponents were able to capture the belt from Flair at various times, but the Nature Boy kept regaining his title.

The master of the figure-four leg-lock, "Flair is never too far away from a world title," said wrestler Arn Anderson. "Don't ever sell him short!"

Ric is a charter member of the "Four Horsemen," wrestling's elite group of villains who live by the credo, "all for one and one for all."

Through the years he has been managed by J. J. Dillon, Hiro Matsuda and Woman. Main events featuring Flair against Lex Luger, Sting, Terry Funk and Ricky Steamboat have all gone down in wrestling history as the greatest the sport can ever produce.

"I'm the 60-minute man," said Flair. "Whether you like me or you don't, learn to love me, because I am the greatest there is."

LEFT: *The Nature Boy in one of his custom-made $10,000 robes. Called by many experts the greatest wrestler of all time, Flair has had the "ten pounds of gold" around his waist many times. "If anyone wants my belt, they have to walk that aisle and climb space mountain. To be the man you have to beat the man," Flair warns his challengers.*

RIGHT: *Flair has Lex Luger trapped in the corner, and takes advantage by pounding his fist into Luger's forehead. These two have battled in front of sold-out arenas all around the world.*

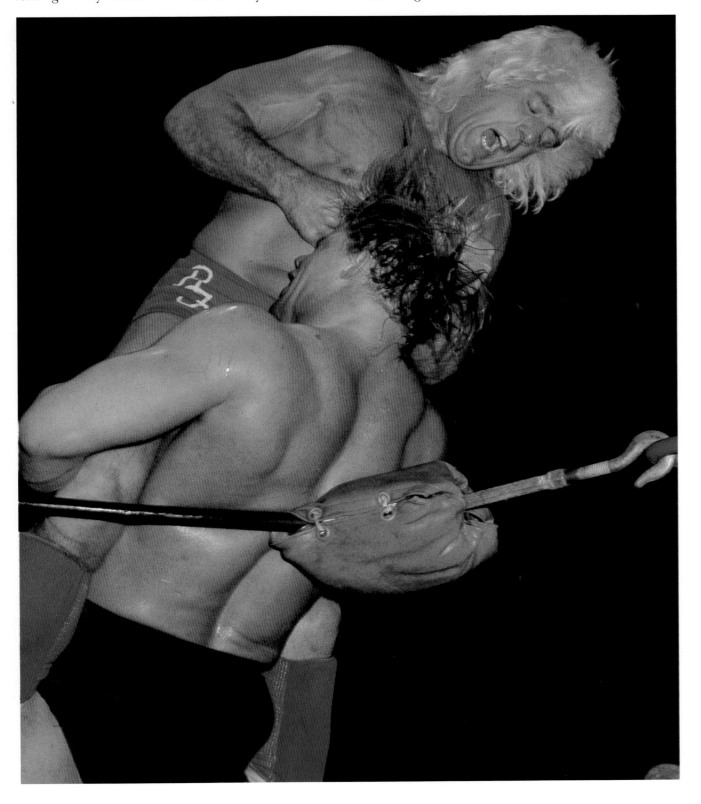

LEFT: *Ric has Lex Luger crying out in pain while trapped in the feared figure-four leg-lock. This hold has been used by many wrestlers, but no one has won more victories using it than has Ric Flair!*

BOTTOM LEFT: *Flair has beaten bigger and stronger men than himself. Here he prepares to slug Lex Luger right in the jaw. He may break the rules, but Flair says, "This is not a sport for the weak. Only real men can survive. And only the very best ever rise to the top!"*

RIGHT: *Ric Flair awaits his next opponent in the ring. He never doubts that he will be victorious. He describes himself best: "I am a jet-flying, limousine-riding, kiss-stealing, wheeling-dealing son of a gun."*

Randy Savage

Randy Savage has been called the Macho Man and the Macho King for many years. He has been the WWF Intercontinental and World Champion. Always the center of controversy, Savage has been both a fan favorite and an evil rulebreaker.

Managed by the lovely Miss Elizabeth for a few years and then by Sensational Sherri, the Macho Man has never run from a challenge. His athletic ability and ring acumen have helped this Sarasota, Florida, resident garner a winning record.

He started wrestling in the Memphis area, where he often teamed with his brother, Lanny Poffo. He worked his way up the ranks and rose to national prominence in 1986. Since that time, the 6' tall, 240-pounder has had major feuds with Ricky Steamboat, Dusty Rhodes, Hulk Hogan and the Ultimate Warrior.

His flying elbow off of the top rope has led to hundreds of victories. "Oh, yeah! Macho Madness is where it's at," he said.

Savage has an unpredictable ring style, but what is predictable is that the Macho Man will continue to be a superstar for years to come.

TOP: *The Macho Man in all his glory! "I am the most colorful and dynamic star in all of wrestling," says Mr. Savage. His boast was made before the Ultimate Warrior forced him into temporary retirement.*

ABOVE: *Savage chokes fan favorite Tito Santana. "Rulebook, what rulebook?" asks Randy.*

RIGHT: *Savage attacks the Hulkster outside of the ring. "Oh yeah, when the Madness meets the Mania – that will be something," said Savage, referring to Macho Madness and Hulkamania. Hogan did defeat Savage at Wrestlemania V, but the Macho Man remains a super star of wrestling.*

LEFT: *Sting climbs the steel cage in an attempt to overtake Terry Funk at the Halloween Havoc event.*

TOP RIGHT: *Champagne flies at the backstage celebration following the Stinger's victory over Ric Flair to capture his first World Title, on July 7, 1990, at the Great American Bash held in Baltimore, Maryland. At the mike Gordon Solie gets drenched as he attempts an interview.*

NEAR BOTTOM RIGHT: *Sting hammers Dangerous Danny Spivey at the corner turnbuckle.*

FAR BOTTOM RIGHT: *Sting displays what was his proudest possession: the World Class Wrestling Championship belt. He lost the belt back to Ric Flair at the Meadowlands in New Jersey in January 1991.*

Sting

Sting. One name says it all. The 6'2" tall, 255-pound high-flying grappler from Venice Beach, California, has worked hard to earn his rightful place at the top.

He began his career alongside the Ultimate Warrior when they were both "Blade Runners." In his rise to the NWA World Championship the Stinger has faced and defeated the toughest men in the sport.

He has been the TV Champion and winner, with partner Lex Luger, of the prestigious Crockett Cup. Videotapes of his many battles against Ric Flair, whom he beat to win the World Belt, are collector's items. His use of the Stinger Splash and the Scorpion Death Lock always guarantee that his matches will be exciting.

Winner of the Iron Man Tournament, Sting is a truly colorful personality with legions of fans who are always on hand to cheer him on. His feuds with the Four Horsemen, Sid Vicious and the Black Scorpion have all tested his athletic ability and personal fortitude to the maximum.

Attacked by Ric Flair and the Four Horsemen and suffering a knee injury that would have ended the career of a lesser man, Sting has come back after major reconstructive surgery stronger than ever! He has several scores to settle and everyone agrees that Sting is the man to do it!

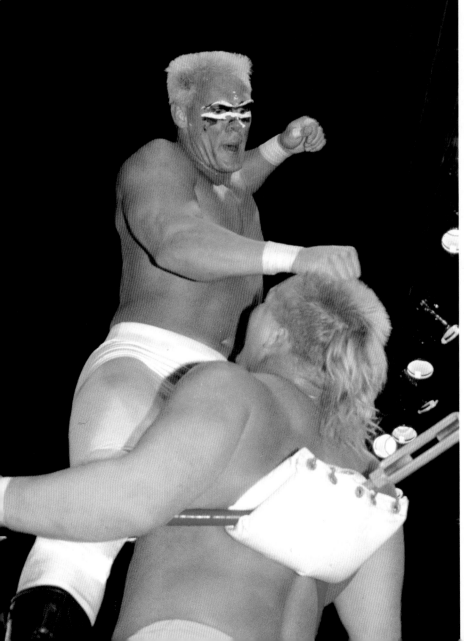

LEFT: *Lex Luger displays his awesome strength as he effortlessly lifts Ric Flair in the air and prepares to toss him clear across the ring!*

RIGHT: *Lex shows off his United States Heavyweight Championship belt. You need more than just muscles to win titles, and Luger has the ring savvy and intelligence to earn the nickname, the "Total Package."*

PAGES 24-25: *In complete control over Ric Flair, Luger asks the fans if he should make a wish!*

Lex Luger

Being billed as the "Total Package" puts a great deal of pressure on a wrestler. Lex Luger has lived up to that claim with little difficulty. The seven-year pro from Chicago, Illinois, has been the NWA Rookie of the Year, Florida Champion, U.S. Champion and winner of the Crockett Cup. His match at the Great American Bash against Ric Flair proved that Luger's time has come. He has made it to the ranks of superstar.

Before embarking on a wrestling career, college and professional football held his attention for a brief period. "Team sports are okay," he told me, "but I like one-on-one competition better."

At 6'5" tall, 275 pounds of rippling muscles, Luger has stood toe-to-toe with the biggest and the baddest opponents that promoters could line up for him.

Luger's 21-inch biceps are a good example of the time and effort he has put into becoming the best possible athlete. His version of the backbreaker is called the Torture Rack, and any wrestler who has experienced it could tell you of the intense pain it causes.

He has had long-running feuds with bad guys Stan Hansen, Sid Vicious and the Andersons, but he has been known to change his ways from time to time. He has heard the cheers of the fans, but he has also strayed from the rule book. Fans wonder if Luger will be faithful to his close buddy Sting, or ignore their friendship for the sake of establishing himself as the brightest star of the future.

"Winning is the name of the game," he said. Perhaps that is a clue to his future. Winning is what he does best!

Ricky Steamboat

Ricky Steamboat is a karate master who often is called the Dragon. He is one of the few wrestlers ever to hold major titles in both the WWF and the NWA. He was the NWA World Champion, the NWA U.S. Champion, and the WWF Intercontinental Champion.

At 6′ tall, 234 pounds, Steamboat is a whirlwind of action in the ring. His electrifying drop kicks and acrobatics in the ring have dazzled the fans for years.

Ricky owns a gym in Charlotte, North Carolina, and obviously spends much time on his conditioning. His reflexes are second to none and his lightning-quick speed have helped in his feuds with Ric Flair, Randy Savage and Lex Luger.

In his appearances on such supercards as Wrestlemania, the Royal Rumble, the Survivor Series, Chicago Heat and the Music City Showdown, Ricky has never let down his fans. His dedication to the sport is unmatched by anyone.

Ricky Steamboat will be one of the major players in wrestling for years to come.

LEFT: *Ricky is all smiles when showing off the NWA World Championship belt he won from Ric Flair!*

BELOW: *Steamboat has Lex Luger in a painful arm lock. Ricky has fought the best in both major leagues and has earned the respect of fans all around the world!*

RIGHT: *Ricky's matches against Ric Flair are considered to be among the most exciting bouts ever held. Here he shows Flair how to fly through the air without an airline ticket!*

Ted DiBiase

Ted DiBiase is the egotistical elitist who says, "Everybody has a price for the Million Dollar Man."

Standing 6'4" tall and weighing 263 pounds, DiBiase is an outstanding wrestler with a full arsenal of ring knowledge regarding holds and moves. Unfortunately, he often takes the shortcut to victory by ordering his bodyguard Virgil to do his work. Sometimes he even bribes his opponents to lose!

Those that don't accept his money are often forced to suffer the humiliation of succumbing to his dreaded "Million Dollar Dream" hold which renders the victim helpless. The evil DiBiase then stuffs $100 bills in their mouths as a sign of his superiority.

The height of pomposity, DiBiase bribed Andre the Giant and ring officials to take the belt away from Hulk Hogan. For a brief moment, he was actually the WWF World Champion until the decision was overruled.

Undaunted, DiBiase continues to have his way in the ring. His feuds with Dusty Rhodes and Jake "the Snake" Roberts have never really been resolved.

The Million Dollar Man, who lives in Palm Springs, California, had his own Million Dollar Championship Belt made! He figured that if he could not win a belt fair and square, then he would just buy one.

The fans detest him, but Ted DiBiase continues to be one of the superstars in the business.

LEFT: *Steamboat has Flair crying out in pain from a vice-like sleeper hold. Steamboat says: "My matches against Ric Flair were some of my proudest moments."*

RIGHT: *The Million Dollar Man displays the WWF World Championship belt that he bought and paid for! Stripped of the title just eight days later by WWF President Jack Tunney, Ted still continues to bribe people to take the easy way out! The fans hope that his bodyguard, Virgil, has seen the light and will never again serve the wishes of the evil DiBiase.*

ABOVE: *DiBiase wrings the arm of Jake "the Snake" Roberts. The fans may despise him because of his egotistical ways, but DiBiase is recognized as one of the great scientific wrestlers when he wants to be. If only he would use his abilities more and his money less!*

RIGHT: *That memorable night on NBC's prime-time Main Event, on February 5, 1988, when Andre the Giant gave the belt to the Million Dollar Man. Ted had paid off the evil twin referee and Andre to beat Hulk Hogan in front of millions on live television.*

Curt Hennig

Everyone agrees that Curt Hennig is an outstanding athlete who knows his way around a wrestling ring. The 6'2" tall, 248-pounder from Minnesota who was the AWA World Champion and the WWF Intercontinental Champion surely is capable of great things. Why does he align himself with bad guy managers like the Genius and Bobby Heenan, and break all the rules when he could probably win matches without resorting to cheating?

Nobody knows what motivates "Mr. Perfect." Creator of the "Perfect Plex," a move which almost always leads to victory, Mr. P has irritated fans ever since his arrival in the WWF.

Like him or not, he rates as one of the best wrestlers anywhere.

ABOVE: *A rare photo of Curt Hennig in his rookie year. Trained by his father, former wrestling great Larry the Axe Hennig, Curt showed signs of talent even way back then!*

RIGHT: *Known today as Mr. Perfect, Hennig displays his cockiness and self-centered attitude as he shows disdain for his opponents and the fans! Wrestling authority Blackjack Brown predicts that Mr. Perfect will see the light and change his ways soon. Let's hope that he is right!*

Barry Windham

Superstar 6′6″ tall, 280-pound Barry Windham from Sweetwater, Texas, has known fame in both major leagues. He has captured such impressive belts as the NWA U.S. Title, the WWF Tag Team Title and the Western Heritage Title. He has been a member of the Four Horsemen and administers the bulldog maneuver like nobody else.

His winning ways put him at the top of his profession, and experts agree that Windham will play an important role in the future of the sport.

ABOVE: *A rare photo of Barry Windham taken during his rookie year. Back then he was known as Black Jack Mulligan, Jr., his hair was darker and he was a few pounds lighter. But all the experts agreed that he would have a bright future.*

RIGHT: *Today Windham is recognized as one of the true superstars in the wrestling world. Championships and accolades are never far away from his grasp.*

33

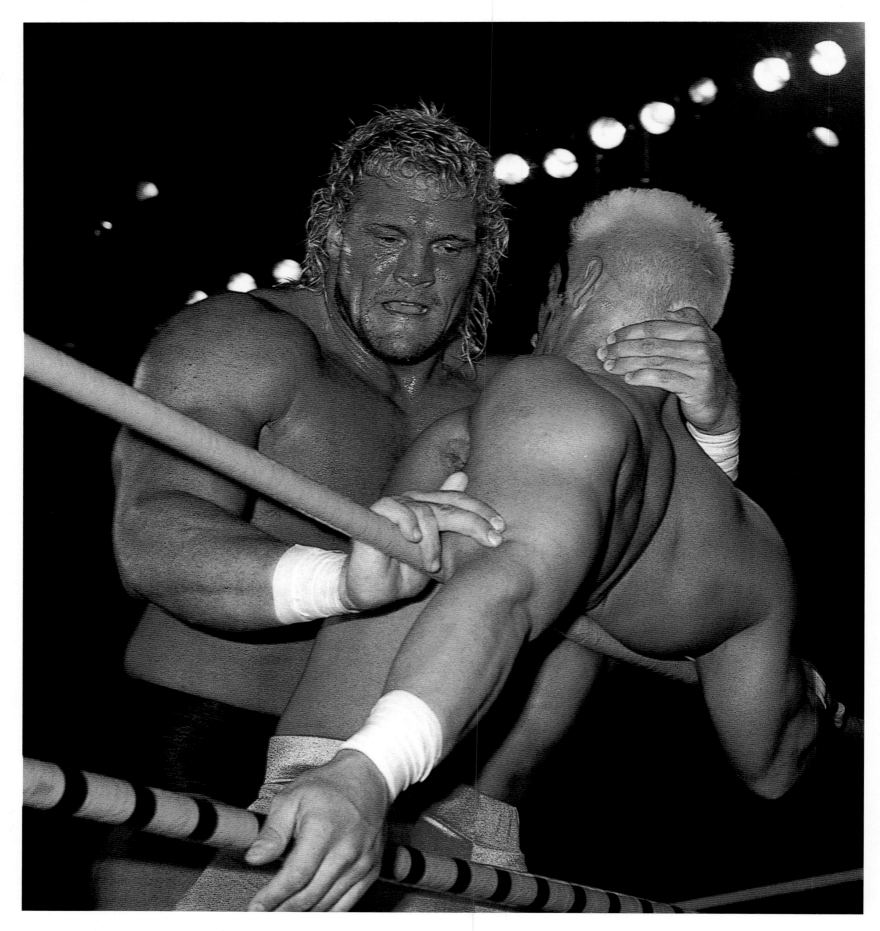

Sid Vicious

Sid Vicious weighs 310 pounds and stands 6'9" tall. In just three short years Vicious has more than made a name for himself, racking up victories wherever he has wrestled.

He deserves to be mentioned in this superstar category because I have no doubts about him being one of the biggest stars in the business. Whether he continues to ignore the rules, or plays by the book, Big Sid is a force to be reckoned with!

ABOVE: *Sid struggles with Sting against the ropes. Vicious is one of the strongest wrestlers in the world. Once a member of the tag team called the Skyscrapers, Big Sid has decided to go solo, and most feel that he made the right decision.*

RIGHT: *Vicious clamps a chin lock on Lex Luger. Sid is actually from Arkansas, but has the unusual ring introduction of, "from any place he damn well pleases . . ."*

Larry Zbyszko and Others

Larry Zbyszko is 5'11" tall and weighs 239 pounds. He has held the AWA World Title and is not afraid of anyone. "I have challenged the so-called champions in every league and no one has taken me up on my offers. In my mind that tells me that they must be scared of me," he told me.

Agree with him or not, the native of Pittsburgh, Pennsylvania, has had an illustrious career and he will play a big part in the future of wrestling.

Other outstanding stars who have made an impact on the wrestling world are Rowdy Roddy Piper, Dusty Rhodes, Kerry Von Erich, the Big Bossman and Jake "the Snake" Roberts. They will all play important roles in the future of wrestling.

Who will be the new superstars? Nobody knows for certain, but it will take a lot of talent to replace anyone in this chapter.

ABOVE: *Zbyszko shows off the AWA World Championship belt. Today he wrestles in the WCW and claims to own his own theme park called "Larryland."*

RIGHT: *Jake "the Snake" Roberts and his best friend, his pet snake, Damien! Most of his opponents are afraid of his snake, but the smart ones are afraid of Jake!*

FAR RIGHT: *The Big Bossman is a former prison guard who takes law and order very seriously. Just ask any of his opponents!*

CHAPTER TWO
THE GROWTH OF WRESTLING

*I*n the eighties professional wrestling came out of the closet and gained the attention of millions of new fans worldwide. Most were people who – before the popularity of pro wrestling in the 1980s – never watched a televised match or even considered attending a live program in their local arena. When rock 'n' roller Cyndi Lauper, Mr. T and others from the entertainment industry joined up, being seen at a wrestling card became chic. Wrestlemania I on March 31, 1985, is generally considered as the turning point in wrestling popularity. Soon new promoters, new and expanded promotional territories and cable television jumped on the bandwagon. Managers, valets and television announcers were as much celebrities as many of the men and women who exchanged holds in the ring.

A pay-per-view concept for special extravaganzas brought the star attractions into homes across the U.S. Network TV helped the tidal wave of wrestling popularity by periodically preempting solid-rated shows in favor of wrestling programming. Wrestlers became as well-known as baseball

and football players. Wrestlemania and Starcade were created by the World Wrestling Federation and the National Wrestling Alliance as their versions of the Super Bowl. In 1987 a record indoor crowd of 93,176 packed the Silverdome in Pontiac, Michigan, to cheer and jeer as Hulk Hogan and Andre the Giant scrapped it out. Pro wrestling had become more than a popular pastime; it was now a big business, too.

The growth of wrestling made stars out of its players. No longer were the wrestlers merely athletes. They could now find outside work because of their own celebrity status. Product endorsements, personal appearances and the very lucrative world of television and film acting were opening up.

LEFT: *The one and only Hulk Hogan. Mike Fleming of* Variety *says, "Without a doubt, the Hulkster is the biggest star that wrestling has ever produced." The Hulkster earns millions of dollars from his various activities, but nothing stops him from giving fans their money's worth whenever he wrestles.*

Hanover Communications in New York was one of the first entertainment agencies to realize the true potential of some of wrestling's biggest stars.

"When we got involved in wrestling virtually none of its major stars had representation," said Lonnie Hanover, president of the firm. "Today, most of the top names have reputable agents handling their contract negotiations and their financial affairs. We treat our wrestling clients the same way we treat our other major league sports stars and our TV and film clients."

No doubt about it, today's wrestlers make more money and are more famous than those in the sport in years past. Wrestling has experienced several years of consistent growth. More live events mean more attendance, and more TV shows

mean more viewers.

There is little debate about who is most directly responsible for making wrestling the sport of the nineties. Hulk Hogan has had an incredible career with so many chapters still to be written. The star of his own movie, *No Holds Barred*, as well as several others, the Hulkster has sold out arenas from coast to coast. Every time he seems to be leaving wrestling to spend more time with his movie career, clamoring fans put on the pressure until he comes back. Hogan has a huge and loyal following. His fans do not fit predictable demographics. They are young and old, male and female, from all ethnic groups and from all socioeconomic backgrounds.

There are certainly other wrestlers who deserve mention because they contributed greatly to the

LEFT: *A true original, Captain Lou Albano has used his fame for worthy causes. He spends most of his free time working for numerous charities. Lou brought a unique brand of showmanship to wrestling, and he has had a lasting impact on the business.*

RIGHT: *Randy Savage has always been in the upper echelon of wrestling superstars. Whether a fan favorite managed by the lovely Elizabeth, or as a villain managed by Sensational Sherri, the Macho Man has always been one of the very top attractions in the business.*

FAR RIGHT: *The son of a plumber, Dusty Rhodes is known as the American Dream. He has been a world champion and one of the top fan favorites through the years. His knowledge of the business and unsurpassed intuitive skills have made him one of the most important behind-the-scenes players. He has played a dramatic role in the past, and will play a vital role in the future of wrestling.*

BOTTOM RIGHT: *Ric Flair has his hands on Lex Luger's neck. For over a decade Flair has had his hands on world championships. He has been the main event attraction for the NWA and the WCW for such a long time, some people may take him for granted. But night after night, Flair puts all of his talents to work in the ring and should be recognized as one of wrestling's most dominant grapplers.*

growth of wrestling. Roddy Piper, Ric Flair, Dusty Rhodes, the Road Warriors, Andre the Giant, Captain Lou Albano, Lex Luger and Randy Savage have all added their own moves, styles, antics and competition to the ring.

While these and countless others will be stars throughout the upcoming years, let's not forget such stars as Superstar Billy Graham, Nick Bockwinkel, Pedro Morales, Ivan Putski, Bruno Sammartino, Bob Backlund and all the others who we cheered and jeered in the not too distant past, and who are no longer active today. These wrestlers helped lay the foundation of the modern mat sport.

And let us also consider some of the great trainers behind the scenes who quietly teach the sport to its future stars. Men like Hiro Matsuda, Afa the Samoan, Dominic DeNucci, Eddie Sharkey, Red Bastein, Killer Kowalski, Billy Robinson, Fabulous Moolah, Verne Gagne, Brad Rhenigans and Pretty Boy Larry Sharpe deserve to share some of the credit.

What can the average fan look forward to in the upcoming years? More spectacular shows on pay-per-view seem assured and more exposure on television also seems guaranteed. This is good news for the fan who cannot get enough of his favorite idols.

Do all the wrestling experts agree? When asked what was in store for the future of the worldwide wrestling sport, Jim Ross of World Championship Wrestling had this to say: "Continued growth!" I couldn't have said it better!

Do you think it is easy to become a professional wrestler? How many months in the gym do you think it took the Ultimate Warrior to attain such a massive body? How many pushups did Kerry Von Erich perform daily to develop his exceptionally chiseled physique? How strict is Sid Vicious' training regimen?

The answers to all these questions can be summed up by saying that it takes years of dedication and hard work in order to build up the body strength enough to succeed in the world of wrestling. Size and strength are just two of the ingredients required to rise to the top of the wrestling business. Today's mat stars must also work on their stamina and endurance.

The travel schedule of the top wrestlers is very demanding. Manager Theodore R. Long told me, "When you are on the road for so many straight days your body pays the price. For instance, your diet is lousy because you have to eat in a lot of restaurants. Second, there can be severe side effects from jet lag. After all, one day we are in Atlanta, and the next day we are in Los Angeles. Third, you are away from your regular gym and sometimes have to settle for unequipped gyms in whatever town you may be in."

Long and his stable of wrestlers try to travel early in the morning so that they can seek out a gym in which to work out by afternoon. "It is important that you never break the routine. If you work out four days a week, then you must always keep that schedule," said Long. "I also see to it that my wrestlers are well stocked in the key vitamins and essential minerals that they need. Not much you can do about restaurant food except to try and order from the healthiest foods on the menu."

Do you want to look like a Road Warrior and join the Legion of Doom (LOD)? It's not easy! It takes more than face paint to look like Animal or Hawk. The two superstars have worked their entire lives to get that unique Road Warrior look. "It started out when we were small," Animal snarled. "Hawk and I were always the toughest on the block and it's because we broke our backs in the gym while others were out shooting pool. We were in the gym every day pushing weights. We knew what we wanted and we worked for it."

I watched a LOD workout at New York's Mid-

City Gym. "This is a hard core gym and not one of those sissy modern gyms," said Hawk. "This place has the same atmosphere as the gyms we go to in Chicago. You know, everyone here is serious about their body, and not about meeting people."

For the next two hours Animal and Hawk worked on their biceps, triceps, pecs, lats, and quads. Their dedication, determination and discipline were evident as they took the time to diligently perform each routine.

Such wrestlers as Tony "Sabba Simba" Atlas, Doug Furnas, Ted Arcidi and Ken Patera have actually won medals for weightlifting. They each

ABOVE: *Hawk pumps iron with his partner, Animal, lending moral support. "We work out as a team, and there are no limits to what we can do," Hawk boasts.*

ABOVE: *Kerry Von Erich, the Texas Tornado, has been working with weights since he was 12 years old. "The more effort I put in while in the gym, the more it pays off in the ring," he said.*

RIGHT: *Hulk Hogan knows fame and fortune, but he also knows the necessity of being in the gym. It is what you call true dedication.*

had a private trainer. On the road wrestling, it is impossible to have a trainer. "You've got to do it yourself. You've got to find the motivation and determination from within," explained Kevin Sullivan, himself a winner of national bodybuilding titles in his weight class. "It is hard not to be distracted by so many things on the road, but you must find the gym and put in the time."

Iron Mike Sharpe is a good example of someone who always has conditioning on his mind. He carries hand grips in his pockets and can usually be found in the locker room doing pushups or situps. "Mike never sits still," said fellow grappler Nikolai Volkoff. "Waiting for your match to occur is a very nervous time. Some of the boys play cards, some watch television. Mike just works out. He stretches, he sweats and he runs in place."

As the story goes, one night after a match Mike Sharpe was working out in the runway of an adjacent locker room. He was so involved in his routine he lost track of time and was actually locked in the building!

IN THE GYM

RIGHT: *Theodore R. Long, manager extraordinaire, practices what he preaches. "If I want my wrestlers to work out hard, I just lead by example," he says.*

FAR RIGHT: *Kevin Sullivan may be a bad guy in the ring, but he knows the value of a good workout. Here is a classic shot of Kevin with the Fallen Angel. Now we know how she got that body!*

BELOW: *Sexy Sindy Paradise doesn't mind when the male fans admire her body. "I want to make sure that they have something special to stare at," she explained.*

BELOW RIGHT: *Flying Brian Pillman feels that it is important that he never lets down his fans. He will sweat in the gym and do everything he can to ensure that he remains one of wrestling's most popular young stars.*

Anyone who watches Mr. Perfect Curt Hennig in the ring recognizes his great conditioning and his excellent endurance. Mr. P wakes up early each morning and goes on a 10-mile run. Sometimes he gives himself Sunday off.

For Mr. Perfect and for other wrestlers, the gym serves several purposes. Wrestlers need to be strong. They need to be mentally tough and determined. They need to possess stamina. A steady workout schedule in the gym can make all the difference in a wrestler's wins and losses records. Generally it is safe to say that the more time the wrestler spends in the gym, the more chance he has of being successful in the ring.

CHAPTER FOUR
THE TAG TEAMS

The Road Warriors

For sheer action and excitement, many fans feel that nothing beats tag team wrestling. Tag team wrestling was very big in the late fifties and early sixties, when such teams as the Graham Brothers, the Bastein Brothers, Mark Lewin and Don Curtis, Antonio Rocca and Miguel Perez, the Tolos Brothers and the Kangaroos ruled the scene. After this initial tag team onslaught, the sport dwindled. Although tag team competition never ceased, it reached a lull in the mid-seventies.

In the mid-eighties, however, tag teams came back strong. Leading the pack was the premier team of the decade, the Road Warriors. Also known as the Legion of Doom, the Road Warriors have dominated both American and Japanese wrestling for almost 10 years now.

From the South Side of Chicago, Hawk and Animal have a combined weight of 570 pounds and have simply squashed whatever competition was in their way.

When manager Precious Paul Ellering introduced the team to the wrestling world in Georgia back in 1983, their debut was spectacular. They had the look of street brawlers clad in leather jackets, and they dealt out punishment during their rookie year like no other team had ever done. They totally were unlike any team that preceded them. They wore face paint and meshed so well together as a unit it was obvious that they had grown up together.

"We came up the hard way on the streets!" Hawk explained. "We like to kick butt!"

Their style in the ring can only be described as brutal. They do not care about the rules and are not above stomping, kicking, double-teaming an opponent, or even ignoring the referee. These tactics would normally be booed by the fans, but Hawk and Animal are such an awesome team that the fans like them.

"They can brawl better than anyone in the business," said Precious Paul Ellering, "but they also can deliver some of the most difficult and elaborate wrestling holds and moves."

Indeed. Hawk has been known to climb to the top corner turnbuckle and fly through the air with

an extended clothesline aimed at a dizzy opponent resting helplessly on Animal's shoulder. Animal can deliver a flying shoulder block with the force of 10 men. They are both heavily muscled men, yet both can even deliver standing drop kicks!

"In the beginning people might have thought that they were just muscleheads," Precious Paul Ellering said. "It didn't take long before they realized that they were more than just the greatest physical specimens in wrestling – they were also great wrestlers."

From the moment the fans hear the Legion of Doom's theme song, Black Sabbath's "Iron Man," blasting over the loudspeakers, they know that destruction and devastation are on their way.

The Warriors have fought their way through all sorts of competition. They have beaten hundreds

ABOVE: *Animal presses a 275-pound man over his head like he was a sack of feathers!*

RIGHT: *The Road Warriors – the Legion of Doom – Hawk and Animal. They are two guys that you would not want to get angry!*

of teams, including the Powers of Pain, the Orient Express, Ron Simmons and Butch Reed, the Funks, the Fabulous Ones, and Power and Glory – and the list continues to grow.

One of their biggest feuds was against Demolition. Insiders say that the Demolition team was basically an imitation of the Warriors. They copied the face paint, the leather and even some of the moves. When Hawk and Animal joined the WWF in which Demolition was the reigning champ, people sensed that the Legion of Doom was anxious to humiliate Demolition and expose them as mere second-rate imitators. Hawk and Animal beat Demolition in city after city, and even teamed with then-WWF World Champ the Ultimate Warrior to battle Demolition as a three-man team. Again, the results were the same. The LOD reigned victorious.

The Roadies had experience in three-man teams as well. They captured the NWA World Three-Man Championship along with their partner, Dusty Rhodes.

The list of titles held by the team is a long one. They have held belts in all three major leagues and have won numerous titles. They have been World Champs, U.S. Champs, Trans-Continental Champs and International Champs. One of the trophies they are most proud of is the Crockett Cup. They captured the first Cup and won a million dollars, coming out on top of the 20-team tournament.

Away from the ring the Legion of Doom is also successful. They own a line of sportswear called "Zubas." Fans all around the world have rushed to purchase the clothing worn by their idols.

Hawk and Animal have proven beyond a shadow of a doubt that they have no equals in this sport.

"We dine on danger and we snack on death," said Hawk. "We have beaten every piece of flesh that they have put in front of us. What a rush!"

LEFT: *Hawk treats the Samoan Savage like he was yesterday's garbage! When Road Warrior Hawk says, "We like to kick butt," he means it. With their size and brutal ring style, Hawk and Animal usually overwhelm their opponents.*

ABOVE: *Luke and Butch show the magic of a winning smile! The eccentric New Zealanders may not have very good manners, but they know how to win.*

The Bushwackers

The most unusual tag team in wrestling today is comprised of Butch Miller and Luke Williams. The Bushwackers hail from New Zealand and have had a long and illustrious career as a unit.

They are cousins who have an unorthodox ring style. Their matches often turn into full scale brawls with lots of fighting both in the ring and outside on the cement floor. They have been involved in blood feuds, cage matches, barbed wire matches and even brass knuckles matches.

Originally known as the Kiwis, and later as the Sheepherders, Butch and Luke captured every tag title that existed in their native land, and garnered many European championships as well. They arrived in America about a decade ago and frightened audiences with their sheer lust for blood and brutality. They were hated by the fans, and feared by their opponents.

Jonathan Boyd, Sean Royal and Johnny Ace all carried the New Zealand flag for the team, and none of them was above interfering in a match to help gain a victory.

Things turned around for Butch and Luke in 1990. They joined the WWF and left behind their flag bearers. They took to calling themselves "Bushwackers," and their ring style changed

somewhat. They seemed to be having a better time in the ring. They would yell at the crowd "whooooooooooa," and the crowd would respond. The younger fans took an immediate liking to them and started to imitate their "bushwacker stomp," in which Butch and Luke march around the ring in a commanding style.

The fans saw that deep down this was a lovable pair of eccentric New Zealanders. Butch and Luke have been known to rub each other's heads for luck during a match, and Luke is never sure when Butch will borrow his head to use as a battering ram into the stomach of an opponent.

During interviews they can be seen slobbering over sardines and stuffing their faces with anything they can get their hands on. They may not have good table manners, but they sure know how to win!

They have had several feuds which took a long time to resolve. Their battles against the Orient Express lasted many months before the Bushwackers were able to soundly defeat them.

Rhythm and Blues was another hated team that fought tooth and nail with the Bushies. Power and Glory versus Butch and Luke sold out arenas across the country.

The Bushwackers usually emerge victorious and if they are cheated out of a win you can be sure that they will not be completely satisfied until they get the job done.

The Midnight Express

The Midnight Express, managed by Jim Cornette, is another team that has had a long track record of titles and awards.

Originally Beautiful Bobby Eaton and Dennis Condrey, and later Eaton with Sweet Stan Lane, the Express captured NWA World and U.S. Title Belts.

Eaton possesses great stamina and is recognized as one of greatest scientific wrestlers when he wants to be. However, he often takes the shorter route to success by cheating. Manager Jim Cornette certainly has encouraged his team to do whatever it takes to win matches. He has used his tennis racket as a weapon more than once.

Sweet Stan Lane is a former lifeguard with a superb physique who is the only wrestler ever personally trained by Ric Flair, known to be one of the all-time great technicians of the sport.

"The Midnight Express is the greatest tag team in the history of professional wrestling," Cornette boasted. Many fans agree, and acknowledge that both Eaton and Lane have that special chemistry needed to be a great team.

"You want to know about teamwork?" Manager Cornette asked. "We work out together every day and we are a fine tuned machine. Bobby and Stan each know what the other is going to do even before he does it!"

The Midnights have feuded with the Rock & Roll Express for several years. Will the feud ever

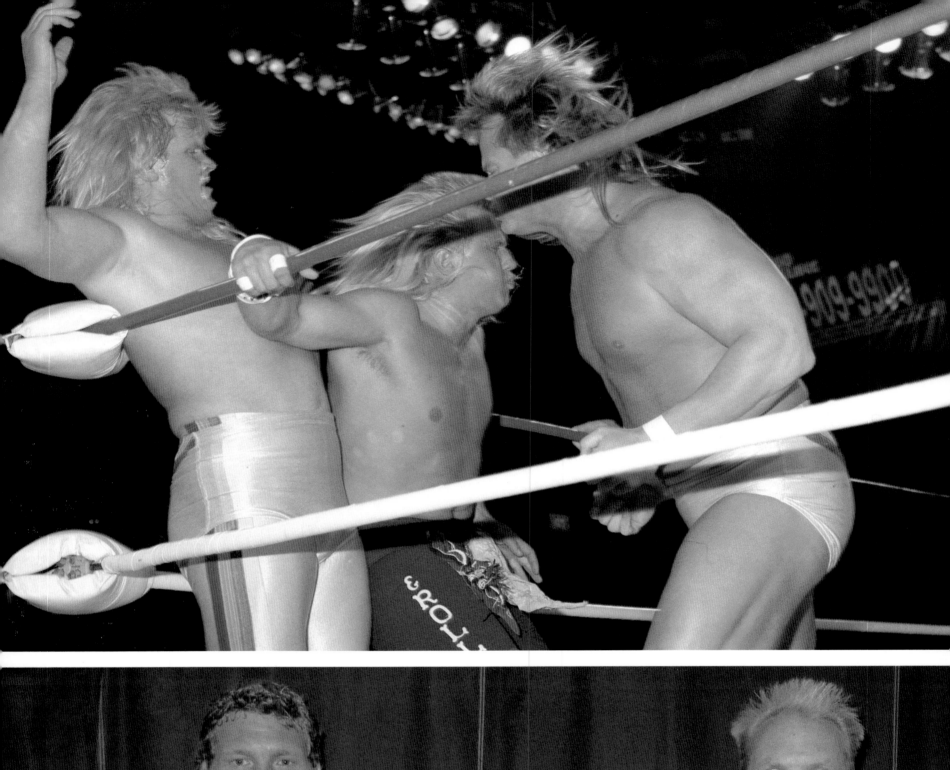

LEFT TOP: *The confrontations between the Midnight Express and the Rock & Roll Express have all been exciting and unpredictable. Both teams have held numerous titles, and each team has beaten the other. Here, Ricky Morton is trapped in the corner by the Midnights.*

ABOVE: *Bobby and Stan show off their gold!*

RIGHT: *Bobby Fulton and Tommy Rogers are the Fantastics, and their long-time feud with the Midnights has electrified fans around the world.*

LEFT: *The deadly combination of Sid Vicious and Danny Spivey – otherwise known as the Skyscrapers – under the guidance of Teddy Long can write their own ticket against most teams, maybe even the Midnights!*

end? Each team holds victories over the other, and the tide continues to roll back and forth.

"Those puny Rock 'n' Rollers will once and for all be eliminated from wrestling by Beautiful Bobby and Sweet Stan," Cornette assured me, waving his tennis racket in the air for emphasis.

Other teams that felt the wrath of the Midnights are Flying Brian Pillman and Tom Zenk, the Southern Boys and the Royal Family.

The Express invented a move called the Vegomatic, in which Eaton jumps off the top rope with a flying elbow into the throat of the opponent who is being flipped in the air by Lane. "It's devastating. Nobody ever gets up," bragged Cornette. You never know when to believe Cornette, but whenever he is talking about the Midnight Express you can be sure that he is not kidding around.

The Nasty Boys

"The Nasty Boys mean business," screamed Brian Knobbs into my ear. "We are meaner, tougher and of course, nastier, than any team that ever existed!"

Big and brawny, Brian Knobbs and Jerry Saggs will never win an award for etiquette. They are brawlers in the true sense of the word. The two Nasties are from New York City, Hell's Kitchen to be precise, and they enjoy hurting people!

"Yeah," said Saggs through a mouth missing several teeth. "We are in the wrestling business for one reason only: to hurt people!"

The Nasty Boys conquered all the competition in the AWA and then won the Florida titles. Later the Boys battled the Steiner Brothers in the NWA and broke every rule in the book. They also broke several chairs and tables which they then used as weapons.

In the WWF, the Nasties went after the Rockers by sneak attacking them repeatedly in city after city. Not only don't these boys play by the rule-book, they don't even acknowledge that one exists!

They are at their best when engaged in a street fight, and they consider every match they wrestle to be a street fight, as their many wounded opponents have found out!

LEFT: *Brian Knobbs has Scott Steiner in a chin lock. The Nasties and the Steiners fought to a no-contest in this brutal cage match!*

TOP RIGHT: *"We didn't get to the top because of our good looks," Jerry Saggs told me. Thanks for clearing that up!*

BOTTOM RIGHT: *The Boys double-team Terry Taylor. "We don't cheat," said Knobbs, "we just win!" Saggs added, "Just ask the Hart Foundation!"*

LEFT: *It's called teamwork! Scott Steiner puts Nasty Boy Saggs on his shoulders and moves him toward the corner, while Rick leaps off the top rope and catches their opponent in a flying bulldog.*

BELOW: *The Steiners are a great tag team. They are also superb individual wrestlers. The question on the minds of the fans is how long before one of the brothers goes after a solo title. Either of them could win the gold!*

The Steiner Brothers

The Steiner Brothers – Rick and Scott – have been the top tag team attraction in the NWA since coming onto the scene more than two years ago to battle the evil forces of Kevin Sullivan and his cadre of villains.

Rick's younger brother Scott was ambushed in the parking lot by Sullivan's bad guys, and because of that attack, the brothers formed their own team to get revenge.

They evened the score with Kevin Sullivan and his nasty men, and then went on to beat all comers to gain the World Tag Titles, and later the coveted U.S. Tag Titles.

Both graduates of the University of Michigan, the brothers were state champions as amateur wrestlers five years apart. Rick entered professional wrestling first, received some bad advice from many people, and became a rulebreaker. He seemed to be under the hypnotic powers of the irresistible, evil "Woman" for a while, but eventually saw the light and turned into a fan favorite by obeying the rules.

Scott is recognized as one of the hottest prospects for superstardom in the business today. He is an amazing athlete and performs moves in the ring which have never been seen before. He is credited with inventing the awesome move known as the "Frankensteiner."

Rick is also one of the greats in the game. Fast and strong in the ring, he was quite successful as a solo star. With his brother Scott they are an incredible combination, and will remain a force to be reckoned with for years to come.

The Hart Foundation

The Hart Foundation is a tag team with a cloudy history. They have been rulebreakers at times and fan favorites at times.

Brett Harte comes from a famous wrestling family. His father and five brothers have all been in the business. He learned to wrestle as a small boy, and his mat skills are outstanding. Jim "The Anvil" Neidhardt is less of a scientific wrestler and more of a power wrestler. Together as a team they have captured the WWF World Titles on more than one occasion.

Originally they were managed by Jimmy Hart, who made them ignore the rulebook and use all the tactics that make bad guy tag teams successful, including lots of double-teaming an opponent and distracting the referee. But they discarded Hart when they found out that he had been cheating them financially. The fans then cheered Brett and Jim for the first time, and it must have felt good. The pair was reborn and finally began to play by the rules.

Demolition had beaten the Foundation, but the Foundation got revenge and beat them to win the title back. With their new image and new formula for success, the Hart Foundation will be part of the tag team scene for years to come.

TOP RIGHT: *Brett Harte has it made in the shade. You can be sure that he will get revenge on the Nasty Boys and any team that treats him wrong!*

RIGHT: *Jim Neidhardt tries to tear Tito Santana's head off! The Anvil has the strength to do it. Fortunately, Tito was able to escape before he lost his head!*

The Rock & Roll Express, and Others

The Rock & Roll Express has the great distinction of holding the prestigious NWA World Tag Team Title four different times during the 1980s. Ricky Morton and Robert Gibson also have the great distinction of being the most popular team among young fans throughout the entire decade. And there is no slowing down for the future. "We will regain those world belts again," Ricky Morton assured me. "Just wait and see. We won't let our fans down."

Their fast-paced ring work makes Ricky and Robert exciting to watch. The duo delivers drop kicks faster than the speed of sound. They are superb scientific grapplers, but they can get rough when the need arises.

They have feuded with the Midnight Express for many years, and have never been known not to face any challenge.

They are also nice guys away from the ring. Gibson uses sign language during interviews because he received a letter from a deaf person, who wondered what he had been saying. Morton is very active in charity work, and regularly visits hospitals to cheer up sick patients.

The agile R & R's have every intention of continuing their winning ways, and nobody doubts that they can.

Several other teams have winning records and the potential for greatness. The Skyscrapers may be planning to reunite at any time. Any combination of the Four Horsemen makes an awesome team. Power and Glory and the Orient Express should continue to be major factors in the tag team wars. Butch Reed and Ron Simmons, the Fantastics, the Youngbloods and the Rockers are all expected to garner winning records. The popularity of tag teaming is sure to continue for years to come.

ABOVE: *Robert and Ricky have some of the most colorful outfits in wrestling. They have a huge and loyal following, and gain new fans with each and every match.*

LEFT: *The Rock & Roll Express show off their prized possession, the NWA World Tag Team Championship belt. "That's what it is all about," Morton said. "With the help of our fans out there, there will be more titles in our future."*

RIGHT: *Gibson puts a hurt on the State Trooper.*

CHAPTER FIVE
THE HIGH FLIERS

Some wrestlers are graced with excellent balance and fearless determination to take any risk to attain victories. They will climb to the top turnbuckle and jump through the air, landing on their opponents. A flying body press or a flying drop kick can be devastating.

Such athletically gifted wrestlers as Sting, Flying Brian Pillman, Macho Man Randy Savage, Superfly Jimmy Snuka, Shane Douglas, Jumping Jim Brunzell, The Cheetah Kid, Leaping Lanny Poffo, Koko B. Ware, Tom Zenk, Marty Janetty, Shawn Michaels, Owen Hart, Ricky Morton, Robert Gibson, Johnny Ace, Bobby Fulton, Tommy Rogers, Bobby Eaton, The Great Muta, Ricky Steamboat, Mil Mascaras, The Guerreros, Kerry Von Erich, Davey Boy Smith and Jeff Jarrett are able to leap through the air and execute all sorts of aerial maneuvers.

The Steiner Brothers are a great tag team, and each brother is capable of performing fantastic flying moves. Rick can attack an opponent with a flying shoulder like no one else. Scott is the master of the Frankensteiner, and the crowd never fails to cheer wildly whenever he catches an opponent in the feared move. The Frankensteiner begins when the opponent is thrown into the ropes, with Scott waiting in the center of the ring for the rebounding wrestler. As he comes off the ropes, Scott flips upside down in the air, catching his opponent around the head with his legs. He then uses the power in his legs and his forward motion to throw the hapless victim upside down onto the mat.

One of the earliest wrestlers to perfect his aerial skills is the legendary Mil Mascaras, "The Man of a Thousand Masks." He has been delivering flying drop kicks and super splashes for over 25 years! Mil has an amazing record of over 5,000 ring victories in his illustrious career, and he has held numerous championship belts. Mil is credited with being the first to use the super splash as a regular maneuver. He would climb to the top corner turnbuckle, stand erect, and then leap across the ring onto his prone opponent. More often than not, this would lead to a three-count!

Strongman Doug Furnas deserves recognition for his ability to leap through the air, despite his muscular body. He possesses a weightlifter's physique, yet he displays the high-flying agility of a much lighter man.

Ric Flair is one of the most gifted wrestlers who possesses prowess in just about every wrestling style. While not often thought of as a "high flier," nonetheless he certainly deserves to be in this category for the amazing knee drops he delivers from midair.

The Undertaker – who was once known as Mean Mark – is 6'10" tall, and despite his giant-like height, he is able to walk the top rope and deliver flying elbows and flying drop kicks.

Ricky Steamboat and his younger brother Vic are both sensational when it comes to flying drop kicks and other aerial maneuvers. Ricky partici-

ABOVE: *Mil Mascaras flies through the air with the greatest of ease! The masked man continues to amaze the fans with his moves.*

RIGHT: *A vintage photo of a bloody Superfly Jimmy Snuka leaping through the air onto a hapless Captain Lou Albano. Bombs away!*

ABOVE: *Rick Steiner pretends that he is Superman! Ric Flair will feel the effects any second now.*

pated in one of the most talked about matches of all time. His battle with Intercontinental Champion Randy Savage at Wrestlemania III was witnessed by millions of people on pay-per-view television, and was a textbook lesson in high flying. Both Steamboat and Savage climbed to the top ropes several times during the grueling 20-minute match. Each used flying drop kicks, flying tackles, flying leg scissors and flying leg drops. This ultimate test of aerial skills resulted in Ricky Steamboat finally rolling Randy up in a small package for the three-count, winning the Intercontinental Championship.

For an average man it would be difficult to live under such a successful brother's shadow, but not for Vic Steamboat. While Ricky was out earning victories and titles, Vic was mentally preparing for his career in the ring. In his rookie year he held an impressive record, and constantly worked to improve his wrestling style. Hard work paid off big for Vic when he captured the ICW World Title, defeating Tony Atlas by using a flying drop kick off the top rope to weaken the muscleman before getting the pin.

Owen Hart once wrestled under a mask when he was known as The Blue Blazer. Owen is the

TOP RIGHT: *When Flying Brian Pillman is in the ring there should be an air traffic controller nearby!*

RIGHT: *Strongman Doug Furnas has amazing agility for his size!*

RIGHT: *Shane Douglas looks like he was shot out of a cannon as he leaps onto Bobby Eaton. Eaton can dish it out, but he also has to take it sometimes! Douglas used to be a Dynamic Dude, now he's just plain dynamic – aerodynamic!*

ABOVE: *The Steiner Brothers show their disregard for the law of gravity. Rick delivers the flying bulldog to Bobby Eaton, who sits on Scott's shoulders.*

younger brother of Brett "The Hitman" Hart, and both of them are capable of high-flying moves. Owen's been known to even fly out of the ring in order to land on an opponent.

Jimmy Snuka was given the name Superfly because of his ability to fly through the air. "Superfly should earn frequent-flyer miles because he is in the air so much," wrestling legend Captain Lou Albano told me. Albano used to manage the career of Snuka, but the two of them wound up as bitter enemies. In a grudge match to settle it all, Albano was hit with a flying Superfly leap from the top turnbuckle and was defeated. "He was tough. I just

wish that he would follow the rules more and be a hero for the fans to look up to," Lou said.

Snuka is also famous for being the first man to deliver a flying body press from the top of a steel cage. At sold-out Madison Square Garden in New York City, Snuka climbed to the top of the 15-foot steel cage in which he and his opponent, Bob Backlund, faced off. Snuka then leaped through the air and landed on Backlund. Controversy surrounds this match because somehow Backlund was able to get up, thanks in part to a very slow official. How can Snuka perform such death-defying moves? He told me, "I grew up on the Fiji Islands, and as a

RIGHT: *Luckily Sting is not scared of heights! Here the Stinger jumps over a flipping Great Muta.*

LEFT: *A hefty 375 pounds of human flesh named Norman comes crashing down! Norman astounds the fans with his aerial abilities, despite his massive size.*

BELOW: *The Great Muta has a terrific sense of direction. He will eventually land on his opponent!*

RIGHT: *The Great Muta hits Hot Stuff Eddie Gilbert right in the kisser with a flying drop kick from the top rope!*

young boy my friends and I would dive off the cliffs into the ocean. Sometimes we would be 100, even 200 feet above the water. Flying in the ring is just natural for me, brother."

Wrestlers have seen the advantages of having agility along with brawn. More and more grapplers are working on their speed and balance. "Once you have been hit with a flying drop kick off the top rope you feel the pain that it can cause. I have been sore all over my body the day after a match with a drop kick specialist," Johnny Ace told me. "I've learned from experience – now I deliver an awesome drop kick from the top rope!"

Fans love to see wrestlers fly through the air. The high-flying style of wrestlers is always fast-paced and extra exciting. Fans marvel at the balance and true athletic skills needed to deliver high-flying action. They know that the wrestlers who climb the ropes to risk life and limb with death-defying leaps through the air are putting themselves in harm's way. The high flyers are more than just finely conditioned athletes. They are truly daredevils!

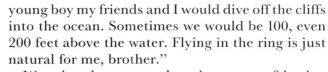

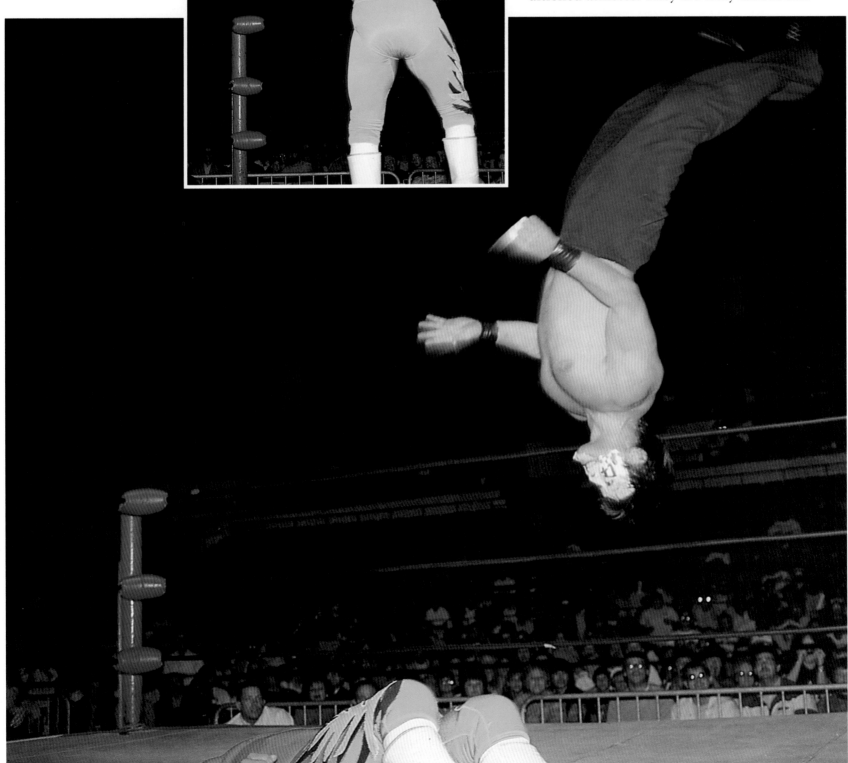

CHAPTER SIX
THE WOMEN

Women's wrestling has a large and boisterous following. The experts agree that for fast-paced action and excitement, you cannot beat watching the battling beauties.

They may be beautiful, but don't make the mistake of selling them short when it comes to physical ability. The top female stars are all great athletes, and they are known for their ability to prove their ring worthiness over and over again.

The current female mat stars never fail to excite the fans, and are gaining in popularity everywhere they wrestle.

There are a few standout female grapplers with tremendous ring victories to their credit. One of the most popular is Misty Blue, from Glens Falls, New York. She has held many solo world titles, and along with sometime partner Heidi Lee Morgan, captured a tag team championship as well.

Misty has been a heroine for the fans to look up to. She always plays by the rules, and represented America in her battles against Russian Comrade Orga and the Iranian Terrorist. "When Misty gets angry she becomes a dynamo of action," said midget wrestler Little Louie. "I've been in some mixed tag team matches with her and seen her up close. If someone gets her dander up they better look out! She can deliver a flying drop kick with as much force as anyone I have ever seen!"

Susan Sexton, who hails from Perth, Australia, has wrestled in over 20 countries and is recognized as one of the greats of the game. She has never paid close attention to the rule book, and she told me, "I am a winner! I always win! I cannot be beat!" While it is true that Sexton has had her way in the ring, many fans feel that too many of her victories have come after illegal deeds, such as grabbing an opponent's hair or using the ring ropes for leverage on a pin. Sexton angrily defends her style: "Look, I am the greatest. I am the best. I know what I am doing and nobody is going to tell me how to wrestle!"

Brandi Mae was born in Spivey, Kansas. Yes, she is a farmer's daughter, and she is absolutely adorable, according to her legions of fans. But she is also ready and willing to face all challengers in the squared circle. Brandi had a long-running feud with Pali Alizar, the Palestinian Terrorist who laid down the gauntlet when she told Brandi that all Americans were inferior to Arabs. "I am from Kansas and no one is going to insult the great people of

this country. We are the home of the brave and the land of the free," said the patriotic Miss Mae. Brandi entered the ring with her hair in pigtails and all the fans were hoping that the farmer's daughter would triumph. The Terrorist disregarded wrestling holds and immediately began throwing punches. But Brandi was wiser; she caught the Terrorist with flying leg scissors and then grapevined her leg for the pin.

Madusa Miceli is a statuesque blonde bombshell originally from Minneapolis, Minnesota, who has risen to the very top of the wrestling ranks. Early in her wrestling career Madusa served as a

ABOVE: *Reggie Bennett, also known as Big Mo, extends Terri Power's arm.*

RIGHT: *Heidi Lee Morgan and Misty Blue display their LPWA World Tag Team Title belts. Known as Team America, they have beaten some nasty challengers.*

THE WOMEN

Misty Blue and Heidi Lee Morgan catch their hapless opponent in a running clothesline maneuver. Misty and Heidi plan to hold on to their tag titles for a long time. "We know how important teamwork is," Misty told me. "We work out four times a week in the gym, practicing moves that will work in the ring." Can't argue with success!

THE WOMEN

RIGHT: *Sensational Susan Sexton with the LPWA World Title belt.*

FAR RIGHT: *Magnificent Mimi says that she should be number one. In the hearts and minds of her fans, she sure is!*

ABOVE: *Madusa Miceli shows off the form that has made her a star around the world.*

ABOVE RIGHT: *Brandi Mae is a sweet girl from down on the farm in Kansas. But don't try crossing her in the ring!*

valet for Curt Hennig in the AWA. She picked up some good wrestling tips from the man who would later be called "Mr. Perfect." She has used her knowledge to gain titles both here and in Japan.

Madusa can be found every day in a gym. "I love it. I don't consider working out to be difficult. It is fun," Madusa told me. Her great conditioning has certainly paid off with ring victories. "I've been the champ in Japan, England and Canada," she boasts ever so slightly, "and I would like to unify all the world belts and become the uncontested ladies' world champion." Madusa has the physical ability and the temperament to do just that. It would be a

RIGHT: *Ashley Kennedy is a knockout with a knockout punch! She has an impressive streak of ring victories!*

FAR RIGHT: *Terri Power has it all: brains, looks and muscles – just what is needed to be a top star!*

74

mistake to bet against it.

The Magnificent Mimi pursues a double career as both an actress and a successful wrestler. She is known for her glamorous ring attire, and more importantly, for her tremendous winning streak which lasted over three years! Mimi lives in Beverly Hills, California, where she is never too far away from Rodeo Drive. "I love to shop," she said, "I am always on the lookout for new exotic outfits."

As an actress Mimi's mat experience has proved an added bonus. "I can do my own stunts better than anyone," she explained. Of course, it is unlikely she will ever be called upon to perform a brain buster in a movie.

Kat Laroux and Linda Dallas, sometimes known as the Nasty Girls, have a reputation for being the toughest and meanest ladies' tag team ever formed. They dress in black, and like their name implies, they will stop at nothing to gain a victory. The fans may boo them, but deep down they know that the Nasty Girls deserve their success in the ring. Kat and Linda are from New Orleans, Loui-

siana, and their close friendship has helped them in the ring. "We know what each other is thinking," explained the Nasty Kat. "We like to double-team our opponents, and I know just the right time to distract the referee," she bragged. Linda also wastes no words. "We cheat, we steal and we break all the rules. We'll do anything necessary to win the match," Linda yelled in my ear.

Perhaps the most unusual lady grappler is Luna Vachon. Luna often comes to the ring with her pet snake wrapped around her body. She has been known to keep half of her head shaven, and rumors persist that she is under the control of some eerie Svengali. "No doubt about it, Luna is weirdo city," said former WWF Ladies' Wrestling Champion Rockin' Robin. "Luna and I have been in some vicious matches. I have been fortunate enough to come away with some victories, but I do not relish the thought of any more rematches."

A few new women wrestlers have broken into the ranks lately. The ones to watch are: Terri Power, Ashley Kennedy, Sindy Paradise and the Badgirl.

ABOVE LEFT: *Nasty Linda Dallas applies a camel clutch on fan favorite Misty Blue.*

ABOVE: *Kat Laroux applies the dreaded Boston Crab and wins one of her many submission victories!*

RIGHT: *Kat Laroux shows that she is not afraid of heights as she comes crashing down from the top rope with a double axe handle, which will hit the poor Oriental Doll right on the noggin!*

CHAPTER SEVEN

WILD, WEIRD, WACKY AND WONDERFUL

*I*f there is one certainty about the world of wrestling, it is that there is no shortage of interesting characters. Wrestlers come from all parts of the globe and in all sizes. Some are natural fan favorites and some are immediately hated by the masses. Many things determine the grapplers' popularity, but no one knows for sure whether a wrestler will be cheered or jeered.

Impossible to classify by type, we call the wrestlers in this chapter the Wild, Weird, Wacky and Wonderful.

No wrestler could be weirder than Kimala, the Ugandan Giant. Some say that the 6'7" tall, 385-pounder, who is a cousin of the Ugandan butcher Idi Amin, is a cannibal who has actually eaten some of his defeated opponents! While no proof exists that these charges are true, I have personally seen Kimala with his own giant-sized crock-pot. What would you expect from a man who carries a spear wherever he goes?

A more gentler giant is El Gigante, by far the tallest man in the history of wrestling. At 7'9" tall and weighing 465 pounds, he was originally drafted by the Atlanta Hawks basketball team. When training, he was spotted by promoters, who knew immediately that his true calling would be in the ring. Even the larger wrestlers in the business are somewhat scared to battle the giant. "He is simply awesome," said Wildfire Tommy Rich. "I would not want to have him as an enemy!" Born in Argentina, El Gigante has been sending most of his wrestling earnings to his family in South America, with the hope of bringing them to the U.S.

Nikolai Volkoff was a despised Russian giant who used to grab the ring announcer's microphone and infuriate the crowd by asking them to sing the Soviet National Anthem. At 6'6" tall and over 300 pounds, Volkoff was always a successful wrestler who broke all the rules and did not care about the fans. When relations between the USSR and the USA became friendlier, Nikolai was one of the first to embrace the Superpowers' friendship. He revoked his Russian citizenship and began waving the American flag. He played it clean in the ring and heard the fans' cheers for the first time. He even received a medal of honor from the Boy Scouts of America!

The Honky Tonk Man is so obsessed with the ghost of Elvis Presley he's convinced that he's the

ABOVE: *Kimala pins Bialo the Giant. Makeup not by Max Factor!*

reincarnation of The King. Along with his manager Jimmy "Mouth of the South" Hart, whom Honky calls the Colonel, the two of them have enraged fans since making their mark in the WWF. Honky insists on singing his so-called hit single, "A Hunka, Hunka Honky Love," whenever there is a microphone nearby. "I am the greatest rock and roll singer of all time," Honky told me.

The Juicer, who is sometimes known as Beetlegeuse, is another wrestler who has a problem with ghosts. He thinks that he is one! At least, the Juicer is a friendly ghost!

The Boston Bad Boy is one of the toughest wrestlers in the business. What makes him so mean? No one knows for sure, but perhaps there is a clue in his background. He was a bouncer in the toughest clubs in Boston's Combat Zone, and rumor has it

that he once tore a man's head clean off during a fight! Sometimes a manager, the Bad Boy forces his stable of wrestlers to follow an unusual diet plan. "I feed them a secret potion from the Orient," he told me. "It makes them mean, just like me!" Nothing like a positive approach to life!

When it comes to unusual training techniques, no one can touch Afa the Wild Samoan. He keeps hungry gators and crocodiles on his farm, and wrestles them to keep himself sharp! "How can any mere mortal not fear me when I have faced vicious maneaters and beaten them?" he explained.

Frankie the Bird is a lot more tame than Afa's crocs, and his owner, Koko B. Ware the Birdman, never goes anywhere without him. "I have taught him to say a few words," said Koko.

"Yeah, Koko! Yeah, Koko!" responded Frankie.

ABOVE LEFT: *Jerry the King Lawler shows off one of the many World Championship belts he has worn.*

ABOVE: *Ron Simmons and Butch Reed used to be close friends when they were known as Doom. This is the way they wanted the fans to appreciate them: as cultured gentlemen.*

LEFT: *Cactus Jack seems right at home in the junkyard. It is not likely that he will make the cover of* Gentlemen's Quarterly *anytime soon!*

ABOVE: *Norman and one of his many friends. I wonder if the two have long, in-depth conversations?*

Cactus Jack is 6′4″ tall and hails from Truth or Consequences, New Mexico. The weirdest thing about Jack is that he seems to feel no pain! "I've seen him land on his head in and out of the ring and he always gets up like nothing happened," said wrestling manager The Braniac. "He sharpens his teeth with a file and he chews on nails." I wonder who his dentist is?

Curly Moe has a great smile and a song in his heart. He weighs 555 pounds and is the nephew of Moe and Curly Howard of Three Stooges fame. Curly Moe celebrates his victories by doing the Curly Shuffle in the center of the ring.

Norman was once called Norman the Lunatic, and he was one of the most ferocious, bloodthirsty heathens ever to set foot in the ring. But somewhere inside this frothing 385-pound monster was a cuddly, kind, gentle giant that was struggling to get out. Today he is a brand new man. Instead of hurtling into the ring with a snarl on his face, he comes carrying a teddy bear. He hugs young fans and never refuses an autograph. Today wrestling fans adore the man they once despised. But be warned, Norman could easily be manipulated, and I would not doubt the words of Norman's former advisor, Kevin Sullivan: "Norman is evil. He has the capacity to maim and kill. I don't believe his new ways for one minute."

Sullivan knows all about evil. He has cast his spell on a dozen wrestlers through the years and somehow manages to get them to do his bidding. "I may have occult powers," he told me, "but maybe people just like me and do things to make me feel happy." Lately Kevin Sullivan has been very happy

LEFT: *Masked man Big Van Vader seems to have unearthly powers, as he causes his shoulder gear to release steam!*

RIGHT: *Luscious Johnny Valiant on stage, performing stand-up comedy. At a recent benefit for MDA hosted by New York disc jockey Freddie Colon, Johnny helped raise $25,000!*

watching so many good guys get beaten up by his men.

One wrestler who has never been beaten up is Big Van Vader. Awesome is the perfect word to describe the reaction he gets from the fans. He's squashed Mr. Saito, El Canek, Jimmy Jam Garvin and Otto Wanz. At 6′3″ tall, 390 pounds, he moves around the ring with the speed and agility of a person considerably lighter. He wears ring attire right out of "Star Wars" and usually enters the ring with a cloud of smoke billowing from the top of his helmet. Talk about a psych job! Is he human?

"I don't know if he is human," said Johnny Valiant, "but I can tell you that he would be good to have around in case you need a battering ram." Valiant, the former WWF World Tag Team Champ and manager of champions, is spending more and more time away from the ring and on stage as a rising comedy star. "Nobody hits back and you don't have to take a shower afterward," Johnny Vee said about his second career.

Another manager who has entered show business is Captain Lou Albano. He is now also known as one of the Mario Brothers on children's TV shows. The Captain holds the managerial record for handling 19 World Tag Team Champions, and has never really left the wrestling business. "It's in my heart, it's in my soul," he told me. "You could ask my doctor, Dr. Rudy Poopufnik, if you don't believe me." Don't worry, Lou. You don't need a note from your doctor!

One wrestler who should visit a doctor – or at least a nutritionist – is Playboy Buddy Rose. The Playboy weighs a gigantic 327 pounds but insists

WILD, WEIRD, WACKY AND WONDERFUL

The Great Muta sprays Hot Stuff Eddie Gilbert with a mysterious green mist during the heat of their battle. The referee was looking away at the time and did not disqualify Muta, but this photo proves beyond any doubt that Muta has been using this unidentified substance against his foes. Gilbert told me after the match, "I was caught off guard. Whatever it is, it burns. But I'm not scared to face him again. I'll be ready next time." Meanwhile, Muta as been wrestling in Japan, where he is winning bout after bout.

FAR LEFT: *Road Warrior Animal in street clothes, with one of his biggest fans, Gregory.*

LEFT: *Sting lets one of his biggest fans, Joseph, hold his World Title belt!*

that he is a fit and trim 217 pounds. "It took years to get this body," he boasted, "and I cannot help it if everybody else is jealous." It is safe to say that the food has not gone to his head, but to his belly.

Another person in serious need of medical attention is Mean Mark, the man they call the Undertaker. This vicious 6'10" tall monster seems to get pleasure from destroying his opponents. He even acts out a mock funeral after his ring victories by placing flowers on his defeated challenger. The

Undertaker might be the one pushing up daisies if he tries that against Hulk Hogan.

There is no doubt as to why Abdullah got the nickname, "the Butcher." The madman from the Sudan seems to rejoice when he sees his opponents in pain. But for a brief moment in time, Abdullah was the "good bogyman" coming out of a mysterious box placed at ringside. It was strange seeing the fans applaud the Butcher, and hopefully Abdullah has seen the light and will permanently

LEFT: *The camera catches Paul E. Dangerously throwing talcum powder into the eyes of James E. Cornette, in a rare manager versus manager match!*

RIGHT: *You can see just how demented the Undertaker is by looking into his eyes! In this street brawl match he attempts to choke out Hawk.*

LEFT: *The Juicer swears that he is a friendly ghost. A team of scientists from the* Weekly World News *are investigating his claims, and have him under surveillance.*

ABOVE: *Paul Orndorff holds Sid Vicious so that the Junk Yard Dog can hit him with his trademarked head butt.*

RIGHT: *Hacksaw Jim Duggan always has his trusty two-by-four nearby. He has used it many times on Sergeant Slaughter.*

change his ways. "Don't be so sure," Mike Rotunda told me, "He is in his own world."

Rotunda is another example of someone in his own world. He still wrestles a full schedule but spends many hours working on his portfolio of stocks and bonds. Along with his assistant Alexandra York, Rotunda seems to be the newest heavy-hitting investor. "Call me Michael Wall Street from now on," he explained.

Cowboy Stan Hansen from Borger, Texas, is not the least bit concerned with the stock market. "As long as I have a wad of tobacco in my chaw and a tank of gas in my pickup truck I am happy," said the easily pleased Hansen. He has other reasons to be happy. He is almost unbeatable in the ring!

Can Leaping Lanny Poffo ever be happy? After years of playing by the rules, Poffo started to call

LEFT: *Second generation wrestlers, the Samoans are more than just unpredictable, they are downright crazy. Here they surround their one-time manager, Sir Oliver Humperdinck, who is now known as Big Daddy Dink.*

RIGHT: *Hot Rod Roddy Piper knows that the show must go on. Just give the man a microphone and step back! Somebody throw Roddy a towel.*

BELOW: *Nasty Boy Jerry Saggs seems to have fallen, and he can't get up!*

himself "The Genius" and wore a graduation robe into the ring. Once the poet laureate of the WWF, Lanny seems unsure of his future. Will he go back to his winning ways, or will he continue on his ego trip?

One wrestler who has no trouble with travel is the 99-pound, 4'5" tall midget wrestler, the Haiti Kid. He was recently attacked by a gang of subway punks but emerged without a scar, leaving the toughs laying on the floor begging for mercy.

"They picked on the wrong guy," said Haiti.

Sunny Beach is a wrestler with an unusual problem. Sunny gets mobbed by female fans wherever he goes. "There is nothing I can do about it," said the 6'2" tall surfer from Santa Monica Beach, California. "It's really not a blessing being so attractive." Now there is a real problem!

Wild, weird, wacky and wonderful. Nobody in Hollywood could create such colorful and dynamic characters.

LEFT: *Tugboat is one of the biggest stars in the WWF. He carries a can of spinach with him at all times! Once a tag team partner of Hulk Hogan, Tugboat wins many matches because of his brute strength and massive size.*

RIGHT: *Nikolai Volkoff squeezes Bam Bam Bigelow. Maybe he's just jealous about those tattoos! Bigelow is one of the biggest American stars in Japan, where he has impressed the entire nation with his ringwork. Volkoff is the former Bolshevik who has seen the light and now carries the American flag to the ring whenever he wrestles.*

CHAPTER EIGHT

FINISHING MANEUVERS

There are some holds and moves which are so painful and inescapable that they force their victims to cry out for mercy and surrender the match. Many of these maneuvers have been around for a long time, but it takes years of practice in order for a wrestler to execute them properly.

Nature Boy Ric Flair is the master of the dreaded figure-four leg-lock. Once caught, few men have ever escaped. Their only chance is to make it over to the ropes and get the referee to break the hold.

Buddy Landel tries to emulate Ric Flair, and copies his style right on down to using the same finishing maneuver. Landel's figure-four leg-lock, however, is much less effective and has been broken by Paul Orndorff, Norman the Junk Yard Dog and Scott Steiner.

The sleeper hold has been used by dozens of grappling greats. When applied correctly, this hold cuts off the flow of blood to the brain, causing its victim to fall asleep. Rowdy Roddy Piper has applied many sleeper holds to gain numerous victories. At Wrestlemania III in the Pontiac Silverdome, 93,176 fans – the largest indoor crowd ever to attend a live wrestling event – saw Piper apply the sleeper hold on Adorable Adrian Adonis. The Adorable One was sound asleep after about 45 seconds of trying to shake off the Scotsman.

After his Wrestlemania appearance Piper took time off from the mat wars to go to Hollywood and star in some movies. Brutus "The Barber" Beefcake then became the most famous wrestler to use the sleeper hold as a finishing maneuver. Beefcake added a special twist. Once his victim was sound asleep, the Beefer would take out his ever-handy

RIGHT: *Nature Boy Ric Flair shows one of the moves that has made him the most respected ring technician for over a decade. This flying knee drop has stopped many an opponent.*

LEFT: *Hot Rod Roddy Piper has Mr. Wonderful Paul Orndorff caught in a sleeper hold. If Orndorff can't make it over to the ropes, he will soon be in dream land.*

shears and administer a haircut!

The Honky Tonk Man was one of the few to escape getting his head shorn by the Barber. Trapped in the hold during a match on national television, Honky used all his might to push Beefcake into the referee, causing an instant disqualification. Even though Honky lost the match by d.q., he saved his flaxen locks! "The Colonel tells me that I can't be a rock 'n' roll star without my hair," said Honky.

Ted DiBiase has developed a slight variation of the sleeper hold which he calls the Million-Dollar Dream. He applies pressure from the side, but the hold is just as effective. Once they are asleep, DiBiase humiliates his victims by jamming $100 bills in their mouths!

Other top stars who regularly use the sleeper hold are Indian Chief Wahoo McDaniel, Dusty Rhodes and Gentleman Chris Adams.

Sting has perfected the scorpion death lock, and

LEFT: *A variation on the piledriver, called a stuff piledriver. As Stan Lane drops to the canvas, Bobby Eaton will drive Ricky Morton's upside down body into the mat headfirst!*

RIGHT: *Sergeant Slaughter rose to the top of the WWF, defeating the Ultimate Warrior for the World Title. Along the way he left dozens of wrestlers hurt by his dreaded camel clutch maneuver. Sergeant Slaughter actually learned the move from the Iron Sheik, who shows the American Turncoat just what pain is.*

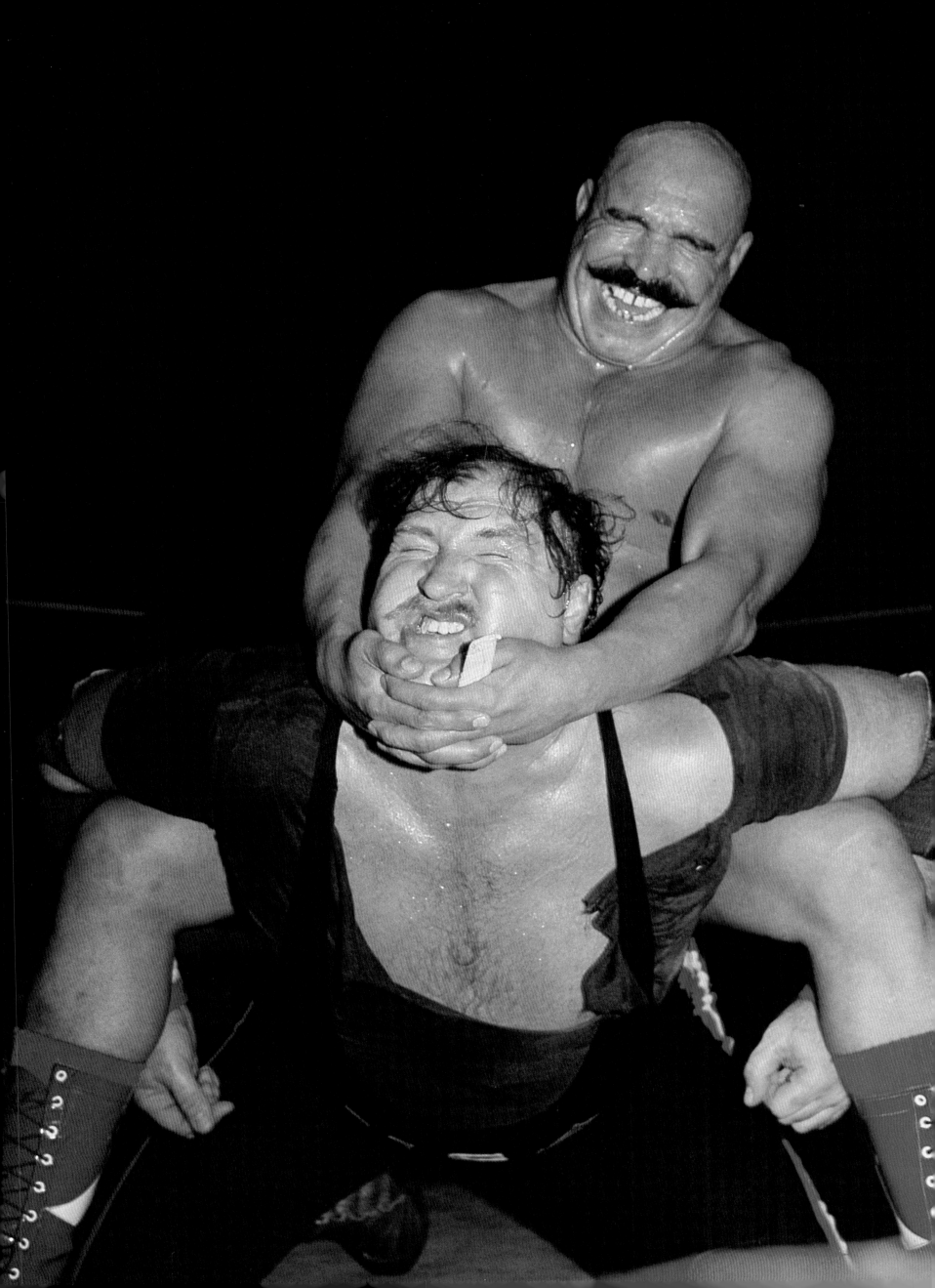

FINISHING MANEUVERS

RIGHT: *Sting applies the scorpion death lock on Ric Flair. "I don't intend to maim or cripple any of my opponents, I just do whatever is necessary to gain a win," explained Sting.*

once he applies it, victory is almost always assured. When the Stinger feels victory is close at hand, he will try to set up an opponent for the scorpion death lock by first hitting him with the Stinger splash. He literally flies through the air, hitting his unlucky opponent with his whole body. After Sting has sufficiently weakened his opponent with this surprise, Sting will grab onto the victim's legs and grapevine them around his, while simultaneously driving the foe's body down to the mat. He then applies pressure on the kneecap by turning counterclockwise with his upper body, causing severe pain.

Sting has made more than 100 wrestlers submit with the death lock, and all the villains who are scheduled to fight Sting spend much of their preparatory time considering escape techniques.

Other holds which often guarantee victory are the abdominal stretch and the camel clutch. Many wrestlers have used the abdominal stretch, but few as effectively as Ricky Steamboat. The camel clutch has figured in many victories for the Iron Sheik, and recently by a former opponent of the Sheik's, Sergeant Slaughter. After being its victim, Slaughter knew firsthand how much pain the hold caused. He learned it, practiced it and perfected it so he could use it on his future enemies.

Many other devastating moves qualify as finishing maneuvers because they weaken the victim. The piledriver, the reverse neck-breaker, the flying shoulder block, the side suplex, the backbreaker, and the flying knee drop can all spell the end of a hard-fought match.

The side suplex has been used effectively by many wrestlers, including Barry Windham, Ace Bob Orton and the Big Bossman. The move is quicker than a full suplex, and is devastating. The victim is rapidly turned upside down and thrown across the ring.

Hulk Hogan caught Bossman in both side and full suplexes during a cage match in the Los Angeles Sports Arena in front of a packed house. Witnesses swear that they could actually see the whole ring move when the two giants landed!

Few wrestlers use the piledriver as often as Paul Orndorff. Mr. Wonderful has racked up hundreds of victories using this lethal weapon.

Whenever the Legion of Doom wrestles, opponents must be wary of Animal's flying shoulder

FINISHING MANEUVERS

LEFT: *Hacksaw Butch Reed lifts Ric Flair high in the air in the gorilla press. Flair will soon be heading toward the mat!*

RIGHT: *The mighty Lex Luger has the Undertaker in the torture rack. This form of the backbreaker can crack a man's spine if he doesn't submit after a few seconds!*

BELOW RIGHT: *Stan the Lariat Hansen drops a flying elbow on a helpless Tom Z-Man Zenk. The bad man from Borger, Texas, is considered by many to be the toughest brawler in all of wrestling.*

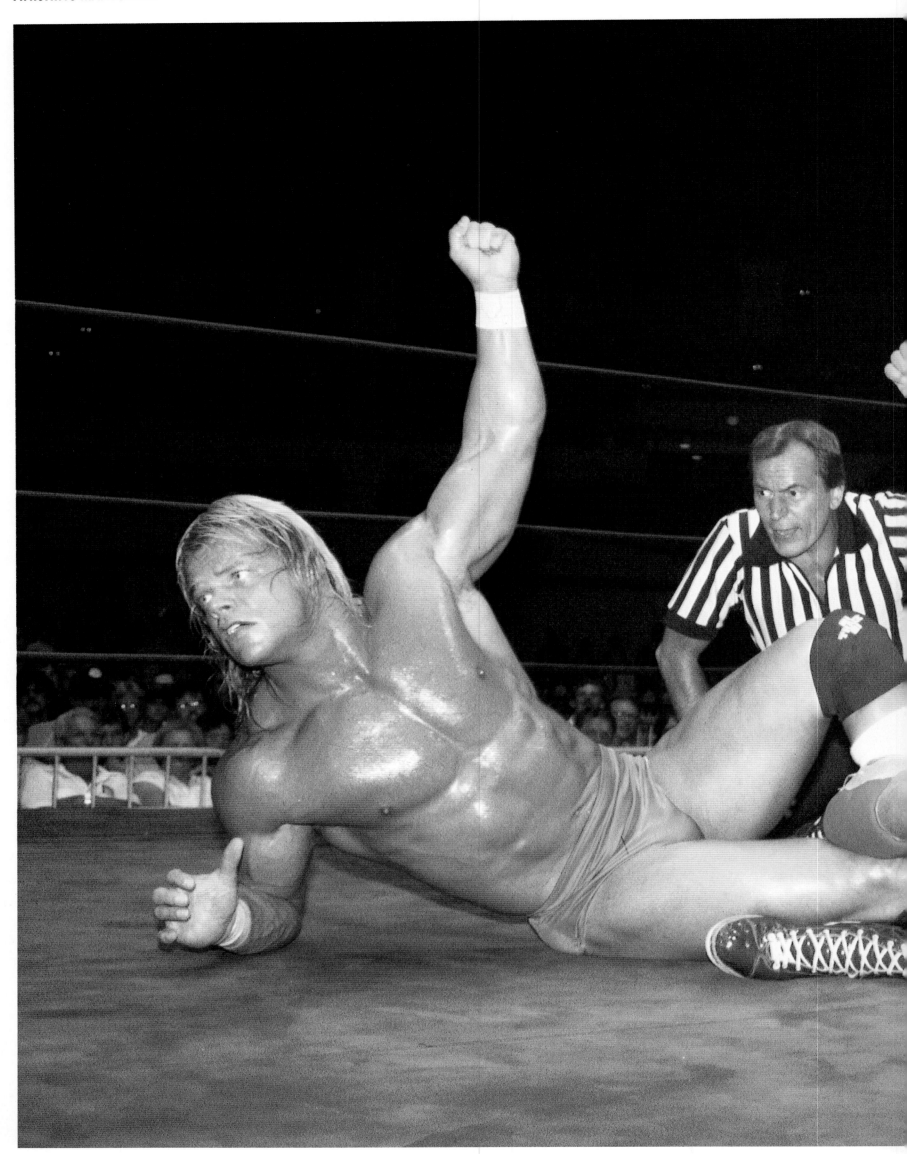

LEFT: *Ric Flair has Lex Luger in the figure-four leg-lock. "It's time to go to school, whoooooo," yells the pompous Flair to the audience.*

block and Hawk's vicious reverse neck-breaker. Either move can ruin their helpless opponents' careers! The Legion defeated three-time WWF World Tag Team Champion Demolition so many times that Demolition was forced to take in new members, and when that was not enough to defeat the Legion, they eventually disbanded!

Hawk and Animal's former manager, Paul Ellering, remarked, "I cannot begin to tell you the number of teams who have quit wrestling after getting a beating by the LOD."

Many grapplers have gained success with the pain-inducing backbreaker. The powerful Lex Luger often uses the backbreaker as a finishing maneuver.

Luger had Ric Flair high in the air and crying out in pain at the main event of WrestleWar. "I thought for sure Luger was going to win the belt that night," said wrestling manager Theodore R. Long. But it was not to be. Luger was distracted when he saw his friend Sting being attacked at ringside by Flair's allies, the Four Horsemen.

Luger let Ric Flair down in order to save his friend Sting, from the brutal sneak attack, and he was counted out of the ring, which allowed Flair to be victorious.

Jake "the Snake" Roberts is the master of another devastating move known as the DDT. He hooks his opponent in a front face-lock and then rams the victim headfirst into the canvas. His foes are usually unconscious after this move. "We have had to revive many wrestlers after the DDT," said an EMS technician, who asked for anonymity.

Fans can expect to see their favorite wrestlers continuing to use the same finishing maneuvers for years to come. Once a wrestler has perfected his own personal weapon, there is little reason to change it. Where will the new moves come from? Nobody knows for certain, but with the wrestlers spending more and more time training, and with the devious minds of such wrestling managers as Bobby Heenan, Slick, Jim Cornette, Jimmy Hart and Mr. Fuji hard at work, new methods of destruction are sure to be found.

ABOVE: *Beautiful Bobby Eaton starts a side suplex which will turn his opponent's world upside down!*

RIGHT: *Hawk snaps the neck of former Doomster Ron Simmons. "I like to hear the sound of the neck snapping!" said the cruel Hawk.*

CHAPTER NINE

AWAY FROM THE RING

*E*veryone knows what their favorite wrestling idols are capable of in the ring. But the typical fan never gets to see his or her favorite grappler outside of the arena.

Like anyone else, wrestlers indulge in a range of pastimes, or even pursue second careers. Michael P. S. Hayes always finds the time for his other love, performing rock 'n' roll. Hayes has recorded several songs, and he likes to jam with his band whenever he can.

Hulk Hogan is another music lover, although he has not been serious about his guitar playing for many years. As a teenager, the Hulkster was in a neighborhood garage band named "Ruckus." When I was in Japan with Hulk he took me to a club that was a hangout for musicians. He was greeted with a standing ovation, and then asked to sit in with the band. They handed him a bass guitar, and he played into the wee hours of the morning.

Greg "The Hammer" Valentine was a member of "Rhythm and Blues" with the Honky Tonk Man, but never seemed to use his guitar for much more than hitting opponents on their heads. "I am the greatest singer of all time," Honky Tonk would tell anyone who would listen. Valentine felt differently. "Let's face it. I am a wrestler, not a singer!" the Hammer announced. This led to a bitter feud, with both former partners using their guitars as weapons.

Madusa Miceli is so popular in the Orient she has recorded albums for her Japanese fans. "I love good old sixties rock and roll," she told me, "and I even know the words to some Beatles tunes in Japanese!"

There are some wrestling stars whose interest is in owning classic automobiles. Paul "Mr. Wonderful" Orndorff owns two custom-made Rolls Royces. Jimmy "Mouth of the South" Hart has a garage full of 1950s convertibles.

Paul E. Dangerously recently created quite a stir at an auto collectors' trade show when he purchased two of the sportscars on display with cash! "The guy walks in here like he owns the place, carrying his portable phone and with two bodyguards," said vintage automobile dealer John Bohan. "He looked like a spoiled brat, hoping people would recognize him. I knew who he was, and I knew that he was rich, but even I was surprised when I saw what was in the metal briefcase

the taller of his two musclemen was carrying. It was full of neatly packaged $50 bills!"

Some of the strongest men in the sport also have a softer side. Ricky "The Dragon" Steamboat is a devoted family man, and often brings his son, Ricky Jr., to the ring with him. I recently accompanied Ricky, his wife, Bonnie, and his son on a cross-country airliner. "I am so proud of my family," Ricky told me. "I want them to be by my side wherever I go. They give me tremendous support. When they are near me I feel all powerful. Nothing can beat me."

Superstar Billy Graham may have been 6′3″ tall, 255 pounds of incredible power, but he also has an artistic talent, and finds that painting relaxes him.

ABOVE: *Greg the Hammer Valentine changed his image by dying his hair from natural blond to jet black for a few weeks. He also took up music. "I can't play this damn thing," he admitted.*

RIGHT: *Michael P. S. Hayes on stage. I asked him what the P. S. stands for. "Purely Sexy!" he answered.*

"I have been working with oil paints and acrylics for a long time now, and I truly enjoy it," the Superstar said. Billy has been told by art experts that he has real potential as an artist. "Frankly, the reason I paint is that it is fun. But if someone wants to exhibit or sell my work, well, that would be fine too," said Graham.

Billy still has a hectic travel schedule even though he has retired from the ring wars. "I travel coast to coast, giving speeches about the dangers of steroids," Billy explained. I witnessed one of Billy's lectures at a university in Ohio. The college students were inspired by his talk, and I can guarantee you that no one who heard the Superstar's story will ever be using steroids. Incidentally, Billy has painted self-portraits which depict his physical condition throughout his battle with the effects of steroid abuse.

Bushwacker Luke Williams loves the ocean and owns boats both in the United States and in his native New Zealand. He participates in speedboat racing, and when in a relaxed mood he enjoys fishing. Judging from the typical Bushwacker diet, he probably catches a lot of sardines.

Woman is one of the most respected managers

ABOVE: *Superstar Billy Graham at the easel. "I used to train by tearing transmissions out of Mack trucks and by ripping the bumpers off of Cadillacs. Today I am into more metaphysical things,"* he says.

LEFT: *Proud papa Ricky Steamboat with his son, Ricky Junior, and his lovely wife, Bonnie. "I credit my family for giving me the desire to be the very best in whatever I do,"* said Steamboat.

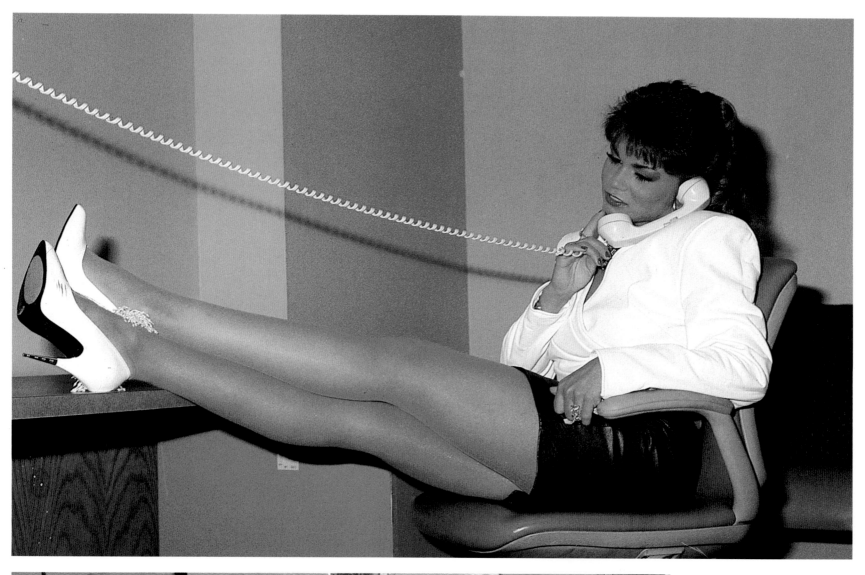

ABOVE: *Woman shows why she was the inspiration for the ZZ Top song, "Legs."*

LEFT: *Bushwacker Luke Williams takes in some sun. G'day, mate. Throw another sardine on the barby!*

in wrestling. Aside from handling wrestling champions, she also controls a worldwide business empire from her executive offices. "She may look soft and feminine," said Lonnie Hanover, a talent agent who has done business with her, "but believe me, she can be brutal in one-on-one negotiations."

If Robert Gibson ever wanted to change his profession, he could become a pool hustler. When he walks into a pool hall or billiards parlor everyone knows that he is a great wrestler, and assumes that he probably isn't too good at pool. They are mistaken. Gibson can shoot a rack of pool as good as the pros. "I saw him beat everyone in the house," said Bobby D'Onfrio of the club, Secrets, in Brooklyn, New York. "He made some unbelievable shots, too."

To be a successful wrestler you must possess numerous athletic skills. Ricky Morton and Barry Windham love to play softball. Wrestling experts know that Windham could have been a professional football player, but most don't know that he also could have played pro baseball. "He would have made an excellent pitcher," major league baseball scout Jeff Greene told me. "With his height and his powerful upper body, Barry would

LEFT: *Mr. Wonderful Paul Orndorff isn't above driving himself around, as long as it's in one of his Rolls Royces!*

BELOW LEFT: *Jimmy Mouth of the South Hart sits behind the wheel of his '59 Caddy.*

BOTTOM LEFT: *Paul E. Dangerously tries on a car for size. If he likes the fit, he'll buy it!*

RIGHT: *Fore! Tony "Sabba Simba" Atlas gets ready to launch a golf ball down the fairway.*

ABOVE: *Barry Windham could have been a big league ballplayer. In the meantime, he's the best hitter on the WCW softball team.*

have been ferocious with a fastball."

Morton was also scouted for pro ball. "Ricky had speed, a good glove, and good reflexes – ideal defensive skills for an infielder. Probably would have been best at second or third base," said Greene. "Offensively, he had a good eye at the plate and had some good power," Greene continued between spits of tobacco juice, "but he wanted to be a wrestler more than anything else, so he passed us by.

"Randy Savage did play a couple of seasons in the minor leagues with the St. Louis Cardinals organization, but he never gave baseball the full attention that it deserved, and so he went on to the ring."

Tony "Sabba Simba" Atlas has bulging muscles from years of gym work and he also has one of the smoothest golf swings you will ever see! Tony and I shot the back nine holes at the Clearwater Country Club where Tony is always a welcome guest. While playing the fairways, Tony reminisced about his long and glorious wrestling career. "I've risen to the top of the wrestling world, winning world belts, titles, trophies . . . you name it. I am good at what I do, and therefore I am good at golf, too!" Atlas scored two under par. My score? Forget it!

Rick Rude may be ravishing, but he is also a champion arm wrestler and has beaten everyone in his weight division! Rude is considered by most to be an arrogant individual. "They don't let him wear those outrageous tights when he competes in arm wrestling. He causes enough excitement with the fans by just walking into the arena," said arm wrestling authority Miles Cane.

RIGHT: *Rick Rude is simply ravishing. Just ask him and he'll tell you!*

INDEX